HALLIDAY'S NEW ORLEANS FOOD EXPLORER

Books by Fred Halliday

Ambler
The Raspberry Tart Affair
The Chocolate Mousse Murders
A Slight Case of Champagne
Halliday's New England Food Explorer

HALLIDAY'S NEW ORLEANS FOOD EXPLORER

Tours for Food Lovers

FRED HALLIDAY

Fodor's Travel Publications, Inc.
New York • Toronto • London • Sydney • Auckland

First Edition

The following recipes are reproduced in Chapter 13 from *Season the Day with Louisiana's Fairs and Festivals,* courtesy of the state of Louisiana: Strawberry Delight, Garfish Balls, Fried Garfish, Orange-Candy Slice Cookie, and Pecan Pralines.

Library of Congress Cataloging-in-Publication Data

Halliday, Fred, 1939–
Halliday's New Orleans food explorer: tours for food lovers / by Fred Halliday. – 1st ed.
p. cm.
Includes index.
ISBN 0–679–02888–9 (pbk.)
1. Restaurants—Louisiana—New Orleans–Guidebooks. 2. Markets—Louisiana–New Orleans—Guidebooks. 3. Cookery, American—Louisiana style. 4. New Orleans (La.)—Guidebooks. I. Title.
TX907.3.L82N437 1996
647.95763'35–dc20 96–23421
CIP

Text Design: Fabrizio La Rocca
Cartographer: David Lindroth, Inc.
Cover Design: Guido Caroti
Cover Photograph: Eugenia Uhl (plate design: Mignon Faget)

PRINTED IN THE UNITED STATES OF AMERICA
10 9 8 7 6 5 4 3 2 1

CONTENTS

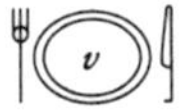

Food for Thought

Among the first sensations that invade the food explorer wandering the streets of the city they call the Big Easy is, At last! Home at last! New Orleans is where haute cuisine hangs out in America. Good food is burned into the consciousness of New Orleanians in ways undreamed of in the rest of America. These people love their food so much that, for example, the first thing an offshore oil crew heading out to a Texas tower in the Gulf of Mexico does, upon taking their station above the Mediterranean-blue waters, is pool their resources to hire a chef to serve them for their tour of duty. Who would leave something as important as dining to a company employee? And the meals had better be good. After dinner, heated food discussions and evaluations rage far into the night, and chefs have been known to leave with a bad taste in their mouths.

With legendary blues and jazz laying down a beat to animate the appetite, you'll find an undercurrent of outstanding food rhythms to fall into step with: Cajun, Creole, Native American, and French. We'll taste the basic New Orleans foods. We'll wander the streets, canebrakes, bayous, and outlying crossroads surrounding the food metropolis, stopping everywhere the nose is arrested or the appetite piqued, sniffing out the best that the American capital of taste has to offer. You will need a car to cover everything. The lush, rewarding countryside just around New Orleans (a drive of less than two hours in most cases) offers immense gustatory pleasures.

Here you'll find food adventures—explorations to the real and historical sources to point you toward the true foods and authentic preparations of New Orleans and the hinterlands whence come much of its produce. Taste routes lead on to more trails, and these lead down byways lined with still more palate adventure.

It was along such a route I stumbled into my first crawfish festival, and so can you. Want to go to a little town on a bayou where the friendliest people in the world hand you crawfish pies, where you can eat jambalaya with them and stay in a cottage overlooking the bayou? Want to enter a big, air-conditioned building in the center of downtown New Orleans and join in a class where you can learn to cook like a Creole and eat all you cook for $20? How about a brewery in a piney woods where no pets are allowed but they put on the dog for you to taste? Would you like to try roast alligator on a stick? "A full 6 inches of genuine gator!" as they say. While dodging the mundane, you'll discover the best in pecan pie and turtle soup, as well as the background history so you can tell the phony from the genuine. The spontaneous leads to mouth-watering discoveries, so don't book your itinerary too far into the future, and keep it open-ended.

In search of food civilizations, we'll travel the Great River Road up the Mississippi just outside New Orleans, into the heart of the old Creole plantation societies and Cajun country. Along these grassy banks lined with cotton and white columns (and oil refineries) you'll continue to the threshold and terminus of Cajun civilization, Lafayette.

Do not shy away from the driving; renting is easy in New Orleans, at the airport or at hotels, and we are talking about forays into moss-draped semitropical bayous on excellent roads where the only encumbrances are the likes of snowy egrets, alligators, and roadside shrimp stands. We travel not only interstate routes, but roads where you will see and taste the most—like the road to Tabasco.

With this Food Explorer we frankly pursue a hunt to find, to taste, and to enjoy the best that New Orleans food (as that elastic term is generally understood) has to offer, wherever it is to be found—be it in a fancy city restaurant, at a Creole fireside, at a food festival featuring strawberries and sugarcane, or in a crunchy and democratic oyster po'boy for sale at a bus stop. The New Orleans Jazz Festival has an extensive food repertory of more than 60 food booths and cooking events on its stages, with samples and demonstrations that cover everything from how to stuff a real Cajun sausage to making sweet-potato cookies. Mardi Gras foods and the specialties of other religious and ethnic festivals are also important, for New Orleans is nothing if not a blending pot of worldwide food traditions.

This is our mission and objective: to find and show authentic New Orleans foods and their styles, enabling you to taste them in the authentic setting of their development and thereby adding to the enjoyment of your discovery. Here, with a smattering of the Cajun, you will sample the credentials of the capital of Creole food culture—its restaurants, from the most glittering and sophisticated to the most honest and basic; sauces and their surprisingly nearby natural sources; food components with matching native and rural condiments. There are also intimate portraits of the little creatures on which we dine—shrimp of all kinds, where to buy 'em, and even catch them alive; oysters, the various kinds, and the whereabouts of the best oyster bars; and the fish of the stream and the sea in which New Orleans, being surrounded by water on three sides, is so incomparably rich.

HALLIDAY'S NEW ORLEANS FOOD EXPLORER

Chapter 1

The "Keys" to the City

New Orleans is a great city for walking around, with plenty of serendipity to see and experience (there's always something happening on the street) on the way to where you're going. Cab dodging, except when you don't know the address or when one of the sudden furious tropical showers hits town, is a sport you can and should play.

For clarity's sake, however, to aid you in moving around, as we list restaurants we will give you their neighborhoods or districts. The city of New Orleans is composed of five major districts and a number of smaller subdivisions.

In the heart of the city, **Downtown,** you'll find the **French Quarter,** the oldest part of town, with the Vieux Carré (Old Square) at its center. It stands in the crook of a bend in the river; every cab driver and hotel keeper knows where it is. All the airport buses unload here. All other directions in town are calculated from here. Also part of Downtown are the **Central Business District** (CBD) and the riverfront. Across the river from Downtown is the West Bank and **Algiers,** where flat-roofed warehouses and factories stretch along deserted streets. It's wise to use a cab in this neighborhood.

The second major district, **Uptown,** lies southwest of Downtown, across Canal Street from the Quarter. Originally a very mucky, hastily constructed thoroughfare, Canal Street was the great divide between the self-sufficient, self-reliant Creoles in the Quarter and the Anglo newcomers who, unwelcomed by the Creoles, settled into the **Garden District,** and up

St. Charles Avenue to the plantation lands that became the **Riverbend** and Carrollton Avenue, where you'll now find a joyful assemblage of funky stores, shops, and restaurants. Many of the street names change from French to English on the uptown side of Canal (Rue Royal becomes St. Charles Avenue, Chartres becomes Camp, and so on). Indeed, Canal was such a cultural divide that the middle of it was referred to as "the neutral ground"; to this day, native New Orleanians call any median along the center of a street "the neutral ground." The St. Charles Avenue streetcar skirts along Uptown.

The three other major districts are **Mid-City,** north of Downtown, and the **Faubourg Marigny** and **Gentilly** farther downriver and east from the Quarter. Miles to the west, between the airport and the Quarter, the vast suburban stretches of **Metairie** and **Kenner** could be Anywhere USA. The way in (and out) is by cab or I–10.

The streets are dangerous, they say, so watch where you walk. Watch it, yes; but, no, don't just sit in your hotel room or take cabs everywhere. By all means, conduct yourself as you would in any big city—go where there are people—but investigate.

For the freshly landed visitor, eager to begin exploration, here are some easily accessible places to land:

CAFÉ DU MONDE
800 Decatur St. (French Quarter)
Tel. 504/525–4544

Across from the Vieux Carré, on the river, this place is unavoidable to the food explorer—the bus from the airport (what you should take from the plane) goes right by it. Here you'll find the best beignets (warm, sugar-dusted French

doughnuts) in the world. To say they are as good as those in France would be to belittle them. And for the coffee, we lift a special cup in its praise. The Café du Monde coffee has the rich, smoky flavor long associated with the dark roast of French coffees wispy with chicory; the powdered sugar of the beignet, which is sure to stay on your lips, adds just the right amount of sweetness to the cup.

Our explorations have put us in the French Quarter. Let's stick to it for our hotel. It's the most interesting part of town and has the most restaurants. Hotel Le Richelieu is nearby; the redbrick residence on Chartres Street was Paul McCartney's address in New Orleans. Le Richelieu is set back from the street with the air of a little mansion. It has its own parking lot and is walking distance from the best restaurants of the Quarter; you can park your car and forget it.

HOTEL LE RICHELIEU

1234 Chartres St. (French Quarter)
New Orleans, LA 70116
Tel. 504/529–2492 or 800/535–9653

The hotel could be on a residential side street in New York or Paris; so discreet are the letters on its marquee you might easily pass by it but for the tricolor and the American flag flapping in soft, creamy breezes. The four floors are carpeted, and the place has a quiet, cushioned feel, comfortable to come home to. The suites have two generous rooms with bath and closets off the bedroom. The mirrors are floor to ceiling, and the furniture is singular. Our suite—the Paul McCartney (No. 227, on the second floor)—was furnished in Chinese Chippendale with a unique armoire from Royal Street, New Orleans's principal antiques market, where you must stroll if you have any interest in beauty and craftsmanship, especially if your taste runs to French antiques.

We were hungry when we arrived but lacked the ambition to set out on a serious food quest so soon, so our hostess, Joanne Kirkpatrick, had prepared for us "a simple luncheon"—burger plate, green salad, and a cocktail. The burger was undressed, plain, and very rare, the salad perfectly dressed and piquant; the drink was a Bloody Mary, a good color choice for the Richelieu (who, of course, wore red), and quite spicy.

Our tongues tingling and spirits revived, we set out for a little walk to get the feel of the streets. New Orleans is a good walking city. The terrain is flat; in the main there are people on the streets at all hours, and they are friendly. As I pass a bar on Chartres Street, a man with a beer bottle in his hand, who has never seen me in his life, smiles and says, "Good morning."

People say good morning all over town. You smile and say good morning back; they expect it from you. You come to expect it; then you start saying good morning first. It's the way New Orleans is, *la politesse de la ville.* The way to enjoy it is to walk. Here in the center of food culture, all you have to do to find a restaurant is take a walk.

For our first important restaurants we are going to select from a New Orleans specialty: seafood. These restaurants are right for easy walking and an easy lunch.

GALATOIRE'S

209 Bourbon St. (French Quarter)
Tel. 504/525–2021

This is an old-fashioned French-Creole sort of place, really a bistro. Plenty of fine food can be put before you, and the ambience is cheerful. The room, brightly painted in gold and green highlights, with plenty of sun streaming past the green curtains, can be noisy and densely packed, but oysters en brochette with bacon are crunchy and briny, classically Creole. Your palate will wonder which taste is which—this is the point of Creole cooking. Galatoire's also does the definitive rémoulade sauce; you can have it with shrimp and some fish. The buttery broiled pompano with warm lumps of crab atop it is something to spoil you—the last bite is lighter than the first. (When a food leaves you hungry, it's a sure sign you've eaten well.) Don't forget to dip shards of the crusty French bread into the melted butter left on your plate; it's traditional at Galatoire's, and the taste is exquisite. If you are really hungry, try the Creole bouillabaisse, a dish spicier in New Orleans than in France. The seafood-stuffed eggplant comes to the table bursting with salty fragrance and things of the sea. Crabmeat Yvonne (crabmeat sautéed with artichoke bottoms, portobello mushrooms, green onions, and parsley) is a specialty here; someone in your party must order it, so that everyone can crowd around the plate with forks when it comes. (Don't fight, however, with forks in your hands.)

There are more than 50 oyster bars in the Big Easy. They are everywhere. Here are some personal choices.

RALPH AND KACOO'S

519 Toulouse St. (French Quarter)
Tel. 504/522–5226

At this large, homey southern Cajun seafood specialist's you can get oysters simple, salty and raw on the half shell. Freshness and evenness are trademarks in the boiled shrimp, the raw oysters, the trout meunière, and the fried seafood platter. The crawfish dishes are served only when the critter is in season. If they are available, take them. This cavernous place, popular with families, is usually crowded and loud.

BOZO'S

31–17 21st St. (Metairie)
Tel. 504/831–8666

From the outside, this place may make you think of Bette Davis's line, "what a dump," but don't judge the book by its cover; Bozo's is not to be missed. For starters, try spicy seasoned shrimp Italian or a zippy-slurpy gumbo. Calorie counters be forewarned; there are really great deep-fried oyster balls—about the size of a golf ball—crunchy and golden.

ACME OYSTER AND SEAFOOD RESTAURANT

724 Iberville St. (French Quarter)
Tel. 504/522–5973

Founded in 1910, this busy seafood house is great if you don't mind the rough edges; you will not be coddled, and the place is as noisy as a Steven Spielberg soundtrack. Chipped-tile floors and neon lights set the tone. Everything from the sea is good here, and oyster is their name; try it in a po'boy (a huge baguette cut lengthwise and slathered with oysters. It's also the place for cool and salty raw oysters (maybe the best in the city). There are wonderful shrimp dishes and, unexpectedly, superb and chewy beans and rice. Long lines prevail at the marble-top oyster bar at lunchtime, for good reason.

Frankie and Johnny's

321 Arabella St., (Uptown)
Tel. 504/899–9146

Great for funky atmosphere (just right for romantics), this neighborhood place right behind the bus barn on Magazine Street has a dusty parking lot. To the left as you walk in the door is a bar that runs almost the length of the large, cool, dark room. The tables are covered in red-and-white checked cloths, the floors are black-and-white check, and there's wood paneling and a jukebox. Here you'll find oyster po'boys; two can try eating from opposite ends. The turtle soup will leave you breathless, too. You can get ice-cold Dixie beer in long-neck bottles. On a sunny day, you can feast in nearby Audubon Park.

For shrimp, try:

Delmonico

1300 St. Charles Ave. (Garden District)
Tel. 504/525–4937

Without an invitation (but call for reservations), where else could you have dinner in a lovely 100-year-old town house in the city's most beautiful district? You can walk from the streetcar past stunning houses; be prepared to be swept away

by the opulence. Delmonico's interior, decorated in earth tones with original art as well as with traditional wallpaper and large prints, is easy on the eyes. Here the shrimp are stuffed, and you will be too. Break yourself in to real New Orleans ways with okra gumbo soup (what! you've never tasted okra before?—change that) and continue with stuffed shrimp or a very tasty, flaky broiled red snapper with crabmeat stuffing. Also try the benchmark jambalaya.

KELSEY'S

3920 General de Gaulle Dr. (Algiers)
Tel. 504/366–6722

You can cross the river by ferry or take the I–90 bridge to get here, and you are rewarded with a shrimp étouffée bursting with the taste of the creature; you'll be surprised to realize that you rarely remember tasting it before. This you won't forget. The seafood gumbo has a deep spicy taste that will have your spoon scraping the bottom. Large plate-glass windows overlook the rather uninteresting neighborhood, but contemporary art on the walls adds considerable color to the room. Prices are easy, but call for reservations.

Mr. B's Bistro

201 Royal St. (French Quarter)
Tel. 504/523–2078

The barbecued shrimp dish here is one of the best. Become a food critic, compare it with Pascal's Manale. All sorts of amusing finger foods, like deep-fried catfish sticks, are very good. The place is laid-back and casually chic, like its guests. For dessert you can have what locals call the best chocolate cake in town.

Palace Café

605 Canal St. (CBD)
Tel. 504/523–1661

An annex of the Commander's Palace, the café is run by the same people, but with very junior prices. The grilled shrimp come with fettuccine, and the menu, with its amusing choices, is a very happy cross of the traditional and today.

Kabby's

2 Poydras St., at the Mississippi River
(in the New Orleans Hilton, Riverside)
Tel. 504/584–3880

In a wood and brick dining room wrapped with windows, here is the best place to go for very close-up views of the Mississippi and its river traffic, as well as the boiled shrimp churning with rich Creole flavors. Dishes from crabs to crawfish bisque are done according to local tradition, too. The place is expensive, but you'll find po'boys on the menu, and the expansive view of the river alone is worth it.

BAYOU RIDGE CAFÉ

437 Esplanade Ave. (Faubourg Marigny)
Tel. 504/949–9912

Try the grilled shrimp with herbed rice and mixed beans; there are three great tastes here, some suffused, and you get an introduction to local food flavors. For something else greater than the sum of its parts, try the ginger-plum brushed salmon, grilled, sizzling, and tingling; it's a taste that is indelible.

PERISTYLE

1041 Dumaine St. (French Quarter)
Tel. 504/593–9535

Only dinner and Friday lunch are served here, but a very creative approach to local abundance reigns in the kitchen. You can try pan-fried oysters with braised fennel and apple bacon relish. Poised like a Greek shrine on its own courtyard, the place is small but very personable, with mirrored walls, candles, and dim lighting.

MIKE'S ON THE AVENUE

628 St. Charles Ave. (Garden District)
Tel. 504/523–1709

Owner Mike Fennelly is a native of San Francisco and the West; his own paintings line the walls. A bright eclectic touch permeates his restaurant and cuisine. Chinese dumplings filled with shrimp, crunchy and spicy, and crawfish-filled spring rolls help to account for the rapid rise to popularity of this Southwestern-Oriental–style restaurant.

DINING ALFRESCO

The Lure and Larder of the Streets

It's hard, as you know by now, to live the sybaritic life 24 hours and three meals a day. It's time to find something simple. Here are some specialties for dining curbside in the New Orleans manner.

PO'BOYS, MUFFULETTAS, ET AL.

New Orleans is famous for sandwiches, and I'm not talking turkey club, baloney on rye and hold the mayo, grilled cheese and tomato, or chili dogs, but po'boys and muffulettas. These are sandwiches you can find only in New Orleans—where else would you find people with the capacity for them? You buy them in a deli or sandwich shop, or maybe a little restaurant with a takeout, take them into the street, and munch them as you walk.

JOHNNY'S PO'BOYS
511 St. Louis St. (French Quarter)
Tel. 504/523–9071

Po'boys are enormous. Eat one and you're set for six hours. Other places might call them subs or heroes, but it's the legendary New Orleans sandwich; stuffing and amount of stuffing make it so. It comes on a crusty French baguette. The loaf is split open lengthwise, buttered and mayoed, and stuffed

with whatever is on hand: ham, roast beef (well done), and gravy is traditional, but cheese, lettuce, and meat balls—bowing to the city's strong Italian influence—are used too; then a futile attempt is made to close it. You see where the name comes from: The financially distressed of the city could make a meal of one of these, and so will you. Here, "dressed" means with lettuce, tomato, and mayo.

THE PROGRESS GROCERY

915 Decatur St. (French Quarter)
Tel. 504/523–1620

CENTRAL GROCERIES

923 Decatur St. (French Quarter)
Tel. 504/523–1620

These are Italian markets, cheek by jowl with each other and across from the French market. Together they comprise an interesting Italian market. In the 1850s Italians moved into the French Quarter and virtually took it over. Stroll the aisles, packed with gleaming bottles of Tuscan olive oil; I found Badia à Coltibuono. Here you'll see rare Italian cheeses hanging over your head. If you have any urban Italian blood in you, and you yearn to sniff the rich odors of Parmesan and provolone mixed, or if you hanker to see mozzarella under water again, or to run your hand through barrels full of dried beans, these two places are mandatory stops. The Central has po'boys for your hunger; local rumor has it, however, that Progress is better for po'boys and has muffulettas that you must try.

A muffuletta is a variation on the po'boy, but it has a unique olive dressing and comes on round Italian bread, sometimes the size of a manhole cover. It can be filled, like the po'boy, with almost anything. The best I know, however, comes with soft-shell crabs and is a gastronome's delight. Call ahead to see whether the blue crabs are in. If they are, don't leave the city without eating a crab muffuletta. Once you have done so, you will take home another one, packed. Like the po'boy, they are great for lunching while walking and seeing the sights alfresco.

So, there you are marching and munching and crunching your bread. Only a short walk up shop- and people-laden Decatur Street is Jackson Square. It's centrally located and has a nice green. The Mississippi's just off to the left, letting the light in, and there are a statue of old Andy Jackson, nice benches, and a wall. You can sit down while you munch. Contemplate the statue of Jackson on his horse and the battle of New Orleans,

which he won—with the help of pirate Jean Lafitte and his men—against the British (after the war of 1812 was officially over; news traveled slowly then). During your ruminations, you will be entertained by all manner of high-quality street performers: musicians, break and tap dancers, acrobats, mimes, and clowns. These performers are licensed by the city but depend on your support to continue their show business careers. The grand edifice overlooking all this is St. Louis Cathedral, built in 1794 and named for the former king and crusade maker of France. It is the oldest active cathedral in the United States.

Diagonally across the street from the church, on the corner of Chartres and St. Ann streets, you can taste the brick-oven-baked cakes and croissants of La Madeleine French bakery (on the ground floor of one of the historic Pontalba Apartment buildings) to finish your lunch, or you can start one from scratch if you haven't had a po'boy or have only been sharing one.

LA MADELEINE FRENCH BAKERY

547 St. Ann St. (French Quarter)
Tel. 504/568–9950

Here is a place that is very close to being authentic. Also, it is unsophisticated and has excellent bread—chewy and yeasty. The decor, in brick and woodwork, is appealing and

businesslike; the products are hot and fresh, service is fast, and you can count on being pleased. Quiches and omelets are featured, soups (onion) are very reasonable; with salad you can expect to satisfy a normal hunger, with coffee, for $9. Wood-fired roast chicken is usually on hand and tasty for more substantial cravings. Also, being French, they know what a *palmier* (sugared puff pastry baked in the shape of a palm leaf) is, but theirs is a little dry. Opt for a croissant instead.

A STREETCAR RIDE

If you happen to be on the other side of the French Quarter, however, nearer St. Charles Avenue, here is another scheme for munching and lunching on the move. It's almost mandatory during your stay that you take a streetcar ride. Armed with your Progress po'boy (why not? many people eat and ride), catch the St. Charles Avenue streetcar at Canal Street. As it runs along the tree-shaded avenue, you will be riding on the oldest extant urban rails in the country past some of the finest mansions and brownstones in town. Cars run inland parallel to the Mississippi along the 13-mile route (it takes about an hour and a half round-trip) at quarter-hour intervals from 7 AM to 8 PM and from after 8 every half hour until midnight. After that, take a cab.

To begin, take the streetcar at the St. Charles/Common Street stop just off Canal Street. If you proceed from the French Quarter, note that Royal Street becomes St. Charles Avenue once it crosses Canal Street. The Common Street stop, marked only by a small yellow sign, is a good place for a pit stop. Here, two doors down from the stop, you'll see Pearl's Restaurant marked with a sign overhanging the street bearing a neon pearl inside an oyster.

PEARL'S RESTAURANT AND OYSTER BAR

119 St. Charles Ave. (CBD)

Tel. 504/525–2901

There is a 21-foot oyster bar. The oysters come from Black Bay, just south of the city in the Gulf, and are professionally shucked and lined up on a tray for you to slide down your throat. Also to be snapped up is some very good Creole food: Crawfish étouffées, fried oysters, and catfish fingers are spicy and delightful. The specialty that everybody comes for, however, is the blackened catfish po'boy. Also handy is New York deli-style stuff: fresh hand-carved turkey (no processed turkey rolls), corned beef, and so on. If Hoppy is here to serve you, count yourself lucky.

Reboarding another St. Charles Avenue streetcar at the Common Street stop and proceeding ahead, note especially the **Robert E. Lee monument** (this is, after all, the South) as the car cruises around Lee Circle. A 7,000-pound bronze statue of the Confederate general stands atop a white marble column, looking north.

As you travel through Lee Circle, also note the **Howard Memorial Library** (601 Howard St., on the circle), now a corporate office. The **Confederate Memorial Hall** (929 Camp St.), which houses the Confederate Museum, the oldest museum in the state, and the **New Zion Baptist Church,** (2319 3rd St.), where Dr. Martin Luther King gained national reputation and a foothold in Louisiana, are out of view but close by. You can visit these on the way back. Another major landmark is **K & B Plaza** (1055 St. Charles Ave.), a modern office tower leavened by the sculpture garden in front that includes works by Henry Moore and Isamu Noguchi.

Starting at Jackson Avenue, the general bucolic tone of the area is sure to charm you. Stately mansions built by Americans who arrived in New Orleans after the Louisiana Purchase in 1803 line both sides of the avenue. You can look at the houses on one side on your trip out and those on the other on the way back. This is the edge of the Garden District. To see it fully, you'll have to get off the streetcar at the Washington Avenue stop and dip into the lavish residential neighborhood, which lies just south of St. Charles Avenue.

Begin by walking southeast toward the river one block down Washington Avenue to Prytania Street. On the left-hand corner is **The Rink** (2727 Prytania St.), the South's first roller rink, built in the 1880s; it now houses a rather loose federation of specialty shops. More interesting for browsers is the nearby **Maple Street Garden District Bookshop** (7523 Maple St., tel. 504/866–4916), with a good assortment of regional and old books, as well as signed copies of books by many Southern writers, including Walker Percy. It's a place frequented by novelist Anne Rice for autographings of her vampire books; maybe you can pick one up. She lives a few blocks away. Across Washington Avenue, on an otherwise nondescript building, is the facade of the historic **Behrman Gym** (1500 Washington Ave.), historic because it was the training headquarters for John ("I can lick any man in the house") L. Sullivan, in preparation for his title fight with James ("Gentleman Jim") Corbett. Don't look too deeply; only Behrman's facade remains here; the gym and the haunting scent of rosin once lurking behind it are gone.

Across Prytania and down a half block back on the other side of Washington Avenue is the restaurant where Creole is king, Commander's Palace. Walking under the restaurant's bright blue-and-white striped awning may fill you with an enthusiasm for testing the argument that Commander's is the best restaurant in the city. Later. For now we have a walk to finish, and another restaurant discovery to make where I assure you your craving will be satisfied, and you can go in as you are.

With the entrance to Commander's Palace behind you, turn left, and left again at the corner onto Coliseum Street. Proceed straight ahead for three blocks to Second Street and turn left again. The walk will give you a good overall picture of the architectural elements of this classic district and its one-time lifestyle. Along Second Street take in the **Schlesinger House** (1427 2nd St.), a definitive example of Greek Revival architecture, so popular in this country between 1830 and 1860, inspired as it was by late-18th-century archaeological discoveries in Greece, American sympathy with the Greek Independence movement of the 1820s, and rejection of British styles after the War of 1812. Cross Prytania Street, turn right, and walk one block down; before you is the **McGehee School for Girls** (2343 Prytania St.). Its style goes Greek one better and is Renaissance Revival. Note the fluted columns, Corinthian capitals, and Florentine window cutouts. Retrace your steps along Prytania Street to Second Avenue; on the northwest corner stands the **Brennan House** (2507 Prytania St.). Again, it's Greek Revival, built by the famous family of restaurateurs. Before this imperial residence you will gain some idea of the wealth that good food creates in a great food capital. From Prytania Street, you can walk a block to St. Charles Avenue and reboard the streetcar.

About 1½ miles up the line, on the right, is **Tara** (5705 St. Charles Ave.). Take a good look, because it's right out of *Gone with the Wind.* The house in the motion picture was a set; this actual Tara was built directly from the plans for the set, an outstanding example of life imitating art. Keep your head turned to the same side of the street because, in the next block, the **Wedding Cake House** (5809 St. Charles Ave.) shows its pretty porticoes and balconies; a more exquisite example of Georgian Colonial Revival architecture—late-19th-century interpretations of 18th-century Georgian building styles of the Atlantic seaboard—is not extant.

Continuing along St. Charles Avenue, you next enter the University District. The Gothic structure on the left is the **St. Charles Avenue Presbyterian Church.** Three blocks farther, on the right, is **Temple Sinai** (6227 St. Charles Ave.), the first Reform Jewish congregation in New Orleans. **Loyola University** (6363 St. Charles Ave.), on the right, is next, taking up the whole block. The Jesuit-run Tudor and Gothic style complex is the largest Catholic university in the South. Next, directly beside Loyola, is **Tulane University** (6823 St. Charles Ave.). The Romanesque style in Tulane's main building, facing the avenue, is repeated in several buildings on the campus behind. The great greensward across from Tulane is **Audubon Park.** Once the plantation of Etienne de Boré, the father of granulated sugar, it is now a 340-acre park with a golf course, a lagoon, swimming, and a fabulous zoo.

Some ways past the park (the church on the left is the **St. Charles Avenue Baptist Church**), the car makes a sharp right turn where St. Charles turns into Carrollton Avenue. To the left is the grassy knoll of the levee—the man-made earthwork that keeps the Mississippi within its banks, it is hoped. You are in the community of Riverbend. But the end of the line is near, and it's time to think of getting off. At the next stop, as you step down, is the white-columned former city hall of what once was the town of Carrollton. Now it seems right to amend this alfresco stroll to take in a fortuitous and serendipitous dining opportunity. Farther back down the avenue is where we are going: It may be indoors, but it's all so charming you'll think you're still outside.

THE CAMELLIA GRILL

626 South Carrollton Ave. (Riverbend)

Tel. 504/866–9573

It was the first diner in New Orleans and remains a great local favorite. It's not hard to see why. The cheerful aspect of the place, on the tree-lined boulevard, with its white-columned portico and white painted porch, is one of country elegance. Inside, a sparkling counter gleams with white place settings: an immaculate plate, silver service, and fan-pleated napkins in front of every stool, of which there are only 29. The Grill is popular; it's first come, first served, and we're lucky some of the stools are empty. There's often a wait. The staff works in the notches of the W-shape counter; we sit along the outside. The waiters, in bow ties and white waistcoats, offer the fastest service in town. Their every movement, from serving sodas to flipping burgers, is accomplished with a flourish and great panache. It gets your attention, as does almost every detail at the Grill. Locals have their favorite waiters and will often request to be seated (and accept a potentially longer wait) in their waiter's section at the counter. The chili has plenty of bite, but what else would you expect of a town with so much Creole in it? The hamburger is the best in town, great beef taste, and they're all quarter-pounders; but it's the omelets that bring the crowds to Camellia Grill. Try the potato and onion with chili and cheese—it's like eating home fries soufléed: plenty of crunch, but light as a feather. If you have room for something else, try the pecan waffles. Speaking of crunch, and butter-sweet burn, there it is. The coffee here isn't recommended (unless you are from England), but finish with the pecan pie: A killer of tangy sensations and snappy back talk, it's the best in the world. Elizabeth Taylor orders her pecan pies from here, wherever she happens to be. An orange or mocha freeze is what you want with it, to gently roll the pie off your palate. The bill is surprisingly low. What's that, you say? You've eaten much worse for much more. So have I.

Catch the St. Charles streetcar again—you know where it is—and stop in on some of the sights you skipped on the way here.

FOOD SHOPPING

Once visited as a place of feasting, New Orleans is a heaven for food shopping as well; some serious food shopping is almost mandatory. There is a surfeit of interesting, indispensable items; in our accounting we will skip what you are likely to find in your home market, or the rest of the country, and stick to the bird in hand.

THE FRENCH MARKET

920 Decatur St. (French Quarter)
Tel. 504/596–3424

This riotous marketplace of delectables is so huge and hectic with crowds coming and going that you can't miss it. An enormous island, perhaps a block wide, expands under the shadow of an elevated roadway. Its edges shelter a hodgepodge of stalls, foodstuffs, and curios; racks of dolls, rows of toy soldiers, scads of apparel (T-shirts and jeans) complement assorted stalls offering fresh pasta, ground coffee, and po'boys.

The sidewalk is awash in fresh produce, the street teeming in greens. Cabbage is stacked higher than an elephant's eye, but stalks of celery are within reach, and softballs of lettuce, too. The best buy in raw food for the traveler to take home? Garlic wreaths, 20 to 30 bulbs strung on a rope to perfume your suitcase. Mixed nuts are good too: Brazils at $4 for a 2-pound bag and plenty of pickings in pistachios and cashews at all prices. Two-pound bags of pecans, marked down from $4, are priced at $3; I make a deal with the seller for two bags for $4. Prices are soft here; don't pay what they ask.

Among the fresh fruits, there are baskets of strawberries big as hen's eggs, plus peaches. You'll see all sorts of squash, onions by the sack, heaps of colorful spices, and stacked cans of coffee. The Café du Monde's is the best.

Inside **Aunt Sally's Praline Shop** (810 Decatur St., tel. 504/524–5107), big ones come at $1 each. An array of hot sauces, Melinda's and private brands, are extolled by the hawkers brandishing bright bottles. ("I made this one myself," croaks one man.) Along the stalls, in barrels, there are field peas, peppers, pinto beans, limas. Banana pepper sauce looks like a good bet, thinks I, and I bag one; so do pepperolio and quail eggs, at $4 for a jar of a dozen. Next, come ranks of Creole mustards (these aren't as hot as you might think) and rows of rémoulade and hot sauces.

The big steals for the northerner, however, are the luscious-looking vine-ripened Creole tomatoes, $2 for a basket of 10. They don't look like they'd travel well, though, and I'd be unpacking seeds from out of my shirts, so I let them go, reasonable as they are, and turn to fresh bananas stacked on pallets.

New Orleans is particularly rich in bananas; it has always been so, and this is a story of how the food culture can spin off surprising benefits. New Orleans is just across the gulf from the coast of Central America, so the Big Easy has always been host to its produce. Coconuts, no problem; they stack. But bananas do not sit so well on the docks in the heavy, sultry climate. Something must be done with them before they rot. Enter bananas Foster. Enterprising people of New Orleans, the restaurant-owning Brennan family in particular, discovered a perfect use for the surfeit of this perishable; they turned it into the opulent dessert that should be required eating for every visitor who enters the environs of the more palatial city restaurants. Bananas Foster, as it is called for a former Brennan's client, is perfect for this city of excesses. The venue for tasting it should be Brennan's; in my opinion, the inventor still does it best. The dish comes to the table as a plate of sliced bananas swimming in rum and banana liqueur and doused

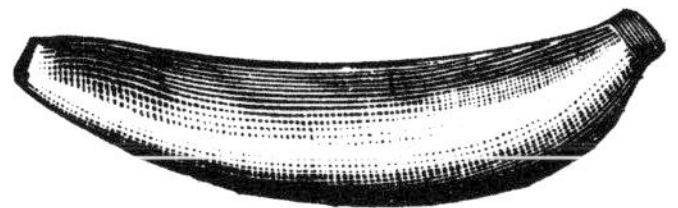

with sugar. Then it is flambéed. Voilà—a rotting embarrassment is turned into a marketable tourist attraction by a creative food idea.

Seafood being one of New Orleans's specialties, you should know how and where to buy it.

Crawfish are a mainstay of Louisiana cooking—the articulated and segmented backbone of that cuisine, in fact. Folks like it in étouffées, in boils, and in pies. Want to try it on your own? At home? Of course. Make your own étouffée; invite friends for a crawfish boil *chez vous* by all means. But buy the critters here, in New Orleans. They are available, alive or boiled, in 40- or 50-pound sacks or smaller, to be shipped by mail, parcel post, or Federal Express like Florida fruit. It is better, however, to shop for your crawfish first at some of the excellent specialty food shops. Establish a rapport, inspect the goods, and set a few ground rules before you buy.

Don't forget to have a blue crab sandwich. It's like breakfast at Brennans, and much cheaper, too. Eat it while walking the streets or sitting in Jackson Square. Eating a soft-shell crab this way is not only delicious but economical; on the average, only 10% to 15% of the entire hard shell crab is edible—the rest is waste; therefore it takes about 10 pounds of crabs to get the amount in the sandwich in your hands (these po'boys are large). Whether you catch your own crabs or buy the meat from the store (lump crab meat is the most desirable; flake means smaller pieces), it is important to remember that it is not a sterile product and even canned, it requires refrigeration at all times. Crabs are available, live or picked, at any of the markets listed below, and the blue crab is common all along the east coast as far as Maine.

To get you started, here are a few addresses where the products you seek can be found.

BATTISTELLA'S SEAFOOD

910 Touro St. (French Quarter)
Tel. 504/949–2724

Although the store is small and crowded inside and not designed to receive tourists, the staff does welcome interested (buying) parties; inspect and ask questions before you buy. That way they will know who you are and you will know what you're getting. Crawfish come by the sack—roughly 35 to 45 pounds. In any case, check out the jars of crawfish fat, an important ingredient to replace (spread it like butter) if you're using frozen crawfish from which the fat has been removed.

SCHWEGMANN'S

5300 Old Gentilly Rd. (Gentilly)
Tel. 504/947–9921

This is the flagship store (255,000 square feet) of the most important chain of supermarkets in New Orleans; they have 12 locations all over town. Indeed, the name has passed into the Creole language: *Je fais une marché à Schwegmanns.* To this day, native New Orleanians say, "I'm going to *make* groceries," using the direct translation from the French. And most of those who speak this way wouldn't dream of shopping anywhere but Schwegmann's. The stores sell and ship sacks of crawfish, live or pre-boiled.

DEANIE'S SEAFOOD

1713 Lake Ave. (Metairie)
Tel. 504/831–4141, 800/662–2586

In a commercial part of town where some of the fishing fleet comes in, Deanie's specializes in and will pack seafood platters laden with crawfish, shrimp, and oysters to your specifications and price range and ship them Federal Express. Go and see what the various platters look like (very appetizing). You can make up your own or order one of the Deanie's standards. They ship crawfish in 40-pound (or other size) sacks, as well as crawfish fat at $8.95 a jar. They also ship oysters by the gallon.

THE LOUISIANA SEAFOOD EXCHANGE

428 Jefferson Hwy. (Jefferson)
Tel. 504/834–9393

Here, on the outskirts of Metairie, you'll find crawfish and shrimp, of course. But it's a good source for pompano and

freshwater fish as well. They ship all over the world. It's a fair piece here from the city; the prices are good, but the merchandise is not on display, so there's not much to see.

For specialty foods—spices, teas, coffees—and utensils, scan the list below. Many hours of happy shopping in the fulfillment of your needs are assured in these stores.

Lucullus

610 Chartres St. (French Quarter)
Tel. 504/528–9620

Aptly named for the Roman emperor who practically invented the art of the feast, this tony place has everything needed to put one on. Lucullus specializes in culinary antiques associated with wining and dining, as well as food-themed art to hang on your walls. There is plenty to see here and browse through—dining-room sets with old walnut tables and chairs, French flatware sets (most of the antiques come from France), many wine gadgets—corkscrews, taste-vins, coasters—dessert spoons and oyster forks, and large serving pieces. All in all a visit to Lucullus is like a visit to a culinary museum.

Riverwalk

1 Poydras St. (Riverfront)
Tel. 504/522–1555

Not to miss: A half-mile-long marketplace starts at this address. Take the Riverfront Streetcar to get here. Many little restaurants and food retailers line the walk; be sure to try local products, such as Evans Creole Candies and Creole delicacies, wherever you see them.

CAFÉ DU MONDE SHOP

800 Decatur St. (French Quarter)
Tel. 504/581–2914

This is a natural shop to enter after the obligatory beignets. Excellent Creole coffee is sold in vacuum tins.

FARMER'S MARKET

North Peters St. (French Quarter)
Tel. 504/52'2–2621

In this adjunct of the French Market, you can buy nuts, pecans, sugarcane, mirlitons (gourds), Creole tomatoes, okra, and garlic wreaths.

GUMBO YA-YA

219 Bourbon St. (French Quarter)
Tel. 504/522–7484

The largest Cajun food and gift shop in the Quarter takes its curious name from a 19th-century Louisiana tattler. Look for Creole pralines, spices, and cookbooks here.

LAURA'S ORIGINAL FUDGE AND PRALINE SHOP

600 Conti St. (French Quarter)
Tel. 504/525–3880

The originals are turned out daily here, and very good pralines and fudge they are. You'll also find a liberal sprinkling of favorite Creole spices.

LOUISIANA PRODUCTS

507 St. Ann St., on Jackson Sq. (French Quarter)
Tel. 504/524–7331

You can order gift boxes filled with Cajun and Creole food items ($10 and up) and have them shipped anywhere.

VIEUX CARRÉ WINE AND SPIRITS

422 Chartres St. (French Quarter)
Tel. 504/568–9463

When you're in town, call about their frequent wine tastings; also stop in for wine by the glass. There is a wide selection of imported and domestic beers, wines, spirits, and cheese, as well as gift baskets.

P. J.'S COFFEE AND TEA

7624 Maple St. (Riverbend)
Tel. 504/866–7031

While you're poking around in this interesting neighborhood, this is the place to take a break. There are imported coffee beans and exotic teas. You can enjoy home-style pastries on an umbrella-covered patio along with fresh-brewed coffees or teas; then you can buy those you like best to take with you—a good deal.

LA CUISINE CLASSIQUE

439 Decatur St. (French Quarter)
Tel. 504/524–0068

Gourmet kitchen merchandise is what you'll find here. Why not? You can browse kitchenware items preselected for value. Don't come here with an idea of what you want fixed rigidly in your mind. They sell what they know, pretested. For example: Le Creuset oven ware (Dutch ovens, roasting dishes, casseroles) are on hand, but top-of-the-range items (skillets, pots, and so on) are not. There is a wide selection of All-Clad, and their top-of-the-line Masterchef is excellent for the top of the stove. Olive-wood and boxwood spoons and spatulas, however, will make you want to cut your vacation short and return to your kitchen. You'll find copper pots, too, and excellent knives. This unbelievably fine selection is fitting for the capital of food.

COFFEE, TEA, OR . . .

630 St. Ann St. (French Quarter)
Tel. 504/522–0830

This place specializes in—you guessed it—coffees, teas, and spices. It's another terrific little watering hole, in a quiet Spanish courtyard as delicious as the tea, yet close to almost everything in the Quarter.

Though Jackson Beer (Jax) is no longer brewed in New Orleans, the old brewery, on the Mississippi riverfront at Jackson Square (Decatur and Toulouse streets), still lingers. Its restoration as an outdoor-indoor shopping and munching mall has made it one of the city's biggest attractions. For the life of me, I can't see why. There are, however, in the hodgepodge of endless shops, bistros, T-shirt emporiums, and ticky-tacky, two stops where you might glean something:

LOUISIANA GENERAL STORE AND NEW ORLEANS SCHOOL OF COOKING

620 Decatur St., Jackson Brewery (French Quarter)
Tel. 504/525–2665

The store approximates the atmosphere of a country emporium. Cartons from factories are set in the aisles, and floor-to-ceiling open shelves are stocked with Louisiana food products. There are Creole mustards, colorful condiments, pepper sauces (buy Louisiana Gold), canned gumbos, and pralines to tempt you. There is also an assortment of cookbooks and Louisiana handicrafts. All in all, you'll find lots to explore if not all to your taste.

Of the several such schools in town, the New Orleans School of Cooking is the best known. Teachers explain and demonstrate the ins and outs of Creole and Cajun cooking in Monday-through-Saturday sessions that last a full morning (reserve ahead). You get to cook, and you eat what you've prepared for lunch: a sure-fire learning experience.

Esplanade Mall

1401 W. Esplanade Ave. (Kenner)
Tel. 504/468–6116

If, after all this, you have some free time, a morning or afternoon, it's worth a visit to this very long stretch of department stores, eateries, and food shops: A branch of Café du Monde is here; so is Semolina, an international pasta bar; and Whole Food Company, a health-food deli plus a complete supermarket for colorful, organically grown foodstuffs.

CHAPTER 4

THE LOAVES AND THE FISHES

Food for the Multitudes

So far we have dwelt on foods for the particular taste, special foods for the picky. Yet, New Orleans has food for the multitudes; the staff of life takes many pleasing shapes, and there is, on a coast surrounded by warm waters baited with shrimp and other chum, the miracle of the fishes—not to mention shrimp and other shellfish.

THE LOAVES

The loaves come from German bakers; in the 18th century, the Germans were invited into New Orleans because of their skill as farmers—for the raising of wheat. The ground was so wet the Acadians couldn't do anything with it. The

Germans came to New Orleans, went 25 miles upriver to a place where they found enough dry land for wheat, and grew it to make a fine farina. So many of them subsequently came over from Europe that the growing community became known as the Côte des Allemands, the German Coast. From growing wheat and milling it, they turned their hand to baking it. Long French baguettes were the accepted shape of the day, so they made them. In the 19th century the best bread in town was made by a bakery called Klotz. Today, much of the bread for po'boy sandwiches comes in paper wrappers bearing the name Leidenheimer. Germans also opened the first breweries and were in on the first experiments with wine producing.

The Germans brought European seed with them, soft-kernel wheat, so the flour they produced was farina. It is the flour used in France and Italy, leading contemporary Americans, returning from those places, to remark on the superiority of the bread. "The bread, the bread," they chant, "it's so good! Why can't we have bread and pasta like that in America?" We don't, as a rule, use farina, or what the French call *blé tendre,* or soft-kernel wheat. Because of the bitter cold in our chief wheat-producing states, hardy hard-kernel (Russian) durum wheat, from which semolina is made, was adapted for use here. It seems we will never make a bread as good as the Europeans until we use soft-kernel wheat for flour.

Louisiana is just about the only state in the United States that produces soft-kernel wheat; the mild climate allows the buds to push through the soft earth in springtime without being nipped by frost. Soft-kernel wheat is thus another happy accident on the Louisiana food scene. Be sure to eat your bread in New Orleans and order ravioli—they taste better here than anywhere else this side of France, because the French continue to use blé tendre. For the shape of their breads, New Orleanians fall back on their Creole traditions and generally follow French forms.

Baguette. The traditional French loaf, it is long and crusty, but light in weight and soft inside.

Ficelle. This is somewhat shorter and much thinner (*ficelle* means "string") than the baguette. A hot one split lengthwise is the ideal companion to good butter and coffee. Try for one slightly burned at the ends. You can find both baguettes and ficelles at **La Madeleine French Bakery** (547 St. Ann St.).

Gigitt. The typical New Orleans bread, as dropped on your plate in better restaurants, is a small, crusty French loaf, often served finger-searing hot. The shape is called "club" or "party" roll in the rest of America, but it is nothing like this. It would be wonderful for hamburgers. For the best, try **Angelo Gendusa's** (1801 N. Rampart St.).

THE FISHES

But people don't live by bread alone. New Orleans is richly endowed with fish and shellfish, which come in remarkable varieties delicate to the taste. There is no way you can appreciate what is set before you unless you understand something of the setting and what it can give. New Orleans is a city virtually surrounded by water. This geographical fact had strong formative consequences for how and what the city's inhabitants eat.

Shrimp. Originally, what native people caught (in the main) around New Orleans was shrimp. Their numbers were prodigious and still are; they are easy to catch. Different varieties of shrimp have different breeding seasons, bringing several runs of shrimp a year. The migrations of shrimp come from the Gulf. With the mild weather the shrimp move up from the bottom to near the surface and through warm water in close to shore, where the nets of the settlers were waiting. They ate—and you will too—principally two types of shrimp: the white and the brown.

The white shrimp is the primary shrimp of the New Orleans area, the one on which the fisheries are based; the one that is sold most often to the restaurants; and, in its larger, adult, second-season, spring phase, the one known as the prawn or jumbo Gulf shrimp. For many years this unimposing creature, about 6 inches long, has been the mainstay of the shrimp industry, which grew out of casual netting on the northern Gulf of Mexico.

White shrimp begin their lives in the waters of the northern Gulf at less than an inch long. In migrations that are as legendary and far reaching as those of the salmon or eel,

they journey to sea as summer advances, returning, with any luck—for the shrimp are tasty to fish, too—by the end of August, having reached 6 inches in length from feeding well wherever they have been.

In any given year, the last young recruits enter the nursery grounds—whence they came—in early fall, bury themselves in the mud, or some other safe, advantageous environment, and wait out the winter. It is these tardy fellows who resume their growth the following spring and reemerge—to be fed upon by schools of pompano, drum, or other fish that migrate to these grounds, and you and me. This returning crop of white shrimp are called "spring shrimp." Their extra season of growth puts them into the bigger prawns and jumbo-shrimp class.

Brown shrimp (including pink shrimp), which grow to 7 to 9 inches and develop closer to shore, are becoming increasingly important in the fisheries and are constantly on the market. Brown shrimp are present on the nursery grounds and in the open sea in all seasons. In their dried form, thousands go to China, a leading customer for U.S. shrimp. The first "brownies," as they are called, hatch early in the year and grow rapidly in the spring. Large movements to the sea take place in June and July, when the brownies are about 5 to 6 inches long.

From early Colonial times, these two shrimp, the white and the brown, were plentiful on the New Orleans market and no doubt supplied a major direction for the creative impulse of Creole cuisine. Indians taught the first settlers to use baited traps and weirs. When the settlers began using nets, brought over from France, the taste for shrimp, and the business of catching it, really took off. In much of Louisiana now there is even a "shrimp course" as part of the meal.

To this day, and perhaps a little more so than in the recent past, we can see one of the more picturesque and favorite pastimes of city dwellers along the sea wall skirting the north side of the city. In the early summer evening, as hundreds of people cast their nets on the warm waters to catch the returning shrimp, spectators by the thousands show up to make deals for the freshest edibles on the spot.

You say you'd like to taste these New Orleans shrimp? That is, of course, the objective of a food exploration. But maybe you'd like to make a deal with a seiner yourself. No, you say. You'd prefer to taste them in a restaurant—but one that does them Creole and uses only the freshest shrimp. Very well, that's possible, too, at a restaurant that grew fat on shrimp.

PASCAL'S MANALE

1828 Napoleon Ave. (Uptown)
Tel. 504/895–4877

On a street just north of St. Charles Avenue, this restaurant became famous for its barbecued shrimp more than 40 years ago. How do you barbecue a shrimp? In Creole cooking barbecued shrimp are jumbo shrimp, kept in their shells (as they are in the south of France), sautéed in a pool of hot butter and olive oil, and encouraged with crushed garlic, chopped peppers, and spices. How do you eat them? With your fingers, taking a bite out of two of New Orleans's greatest legacies—shrimp and Creole-French traditions.

The place is unpretentious; you don't have to wear a jacket. The crowd is local and congenial, and the walls are plastered with posters tracing the history of the restaurant. The prices are fair.

Oysters. To avoid embarrassment, you should follow the one rule on eating in New Orleans; it has to do with oysters. They are eaten standing up—always. Half-shell oysters are laid out on the bar, and you move along slurping them up one by one. You won't be disappointed. The oysters of Louisiana's waters and reefs—farmed and found in the Gulf—are legendary in taste. Their exceptional savory qualities were reported on by early French explorers, but archaeological digs show Indians had been enjoying them much longer than that—for 4,000 years.

Certainly they are enjoyed today. The Louisiana fishery centered around New Orleans gathers 20% of the nation's oyster crop. What is the mysterious something about this briny bivalve that makes it taste so good? To the casual observer the oyster seems to be made of just two sections, the soft body, which we eat as meat, and two outer shells that protect it. But there is much more to it than that. The body is vital and energetic and carries on those processes we describe as life—it takes in food and grows large and fat; it breathes and reproduces. The outer shells are essentially calcium carbonate, but inside them all sorts of interesting things are going on.

The oyster "breathes" much like a fish, in a simple exchange of gases. In their gills and mantle coverings are many small, thin-walled blood vessels. The water the oyster continuously takes in and ejects, flowing around these vessels, gives up some of its oxygen and takes on carbon dioxide. The colorless oxygen-bearing blood of the oyster is pumped through all

OYSTER

parts of its body by its small three-chambered heart. The breathing function of the mantles (on both sides of the body and what we see when we open an oyster) is somewhat secondary. The mantles' primary purpose is to build up the shell that protects the soft body of the oyster.

Now comes a surprise: In addition to its respiratory function, the blood of the oyster is closely related to seawater. The concentrations of salts in the oyster's blood change as the seawater around the oyster changes, yet the proportions of the salts remain the same, and there is a constant ratio of sodium chloride to potassium chloride. The ratio is nearly in the same proportion as that in our blood plasma. No wonder eating oysters is appetizing to us and good for us, too.

But let's go on. Some of the chemicals found in oysters are: vitamins A, B, C, D, and G; phosphates and chlorides, for healthy bones and teeth; carbohydrates; protein in large quantity; and very little (less than 2%) fat. Oysters are an excellent source of iron, so important for the prevention of anemia. They also have a high calcium and iodine content (those from Louisiana have the highest), and their meat contains only 150 calories in half a pound. To contrast, the same amount of red meat contains 700 calories.

Oysters come from many places—almost wherever there is a coastline—but those from Louisiana are carefully watched over by the state, which recognizes only three classifications of the bivalve when offered for sale: steam canned, raw shop, and counter stock.

The steam canned are dredged from the seeded beds of Louisiana. At the cannery they are steamed open; their meats are removed, processed, and placed in cans. These oysters are planned long in advance by shell planting—the factory scatters old shells around the bed; the free-floating young oyster, or spat, falling through the currents lands on the shell, attaches itself to it, and is stuck for life. Two years later, having grown large enough to be brought to the factory, it is harvested. A great majority of oysters canned in Louisiana and Mississippi come from Louisiana's reefs just east of New Orleans.

Raw-shop oysters, on the other hand, require a great deal of cultivation: a virtual underwater farm is established. Independent growers take these oysters from natural reefs, clean and separate them, and place them on bedding grounds leased from the state. Here the oysters take in more food and become better shaped and fatter. The growers then take them up and transport them to packing houses, where they are opened, packed in containers, and shipped under constant refrigeration to all parts of the United States. As many as 15 hand operations are involved in the processing of raw-shop oysters, yet, in all these operations, the oysters are never actually touched.

The counter stock, priced the highest, are oysters of the highest grade. They are the most carefully culled and cultivated oysters and are the type served on the half shell at restaurants and oyster bars nationwide.

Gaining a harvest sounds easier than it is; the oyster has many effective enemies. In Louisiana the conch (or boring snail) is one of the worst. It attaches itself to the oyster, bores a neat hole through its shell, inserts its proboscis and extracts the meat. The fact that this deadly predator must live in water with a high salinity has saved many an oyster bed from total ruin. Nevertheless, fishermen do extensive conch trapping, almost in revenge, offering the animal to the New Orleans market, where it frequently appears.

The saltwater drum fish also causes much damage to the bedding grounds by crushing the oyster shells in its jaws and devouring the meat. These fish, some weighing as much as 60 pounds, gather in large schools and roam far. A bedding ground left to them may be destroyed in a single night—gone are the investment of the lease and all the labor. Fishermen protect their bedding grounds by surrounding them with underwater fences of galvanized wire strong enough to keep out the monster fish.

Notwithstanding, and indeed, perhaps because of this, counter stock oysters in top condition are offered in New Orleans restaurants in a variety of pleasing ways.

ANTOINE'S

713 St. Louis St. (French Quarter)
Tel. 504/581–4422

Come to the oldest restaurant in the city to enjoy their famous creation, invented here—oysters Rockefeller—in a sauce of aromatic greens perked with anise. Its taste is something like eating a garden that was dipped in the sea. At Antoine's, you don't have to eat your oysters standing up.

Arnaud's

813 Bienville St. (French Quarter)
Tel. 504/532–5433

One of the grandest Creole-French restaurants presents a great, creamy oyster stew (now it's more fashionable to say soup, but it's lusciously thick). And faultlessly served.

Broussard's

819 Conti St. (French Quarter)
Tel. 504/581–3866

Oysters are baked here in a definitive version of classic Creole sauce (flour and butter, for the roux, plus onions, garlic, peppers, mustard, and usually tomatoes) with eggplant. The affinity of textures—oyster and eggplant—leaves the palate panting. The setting in two of the dining rooms is lace-curtain Creole—a soft-focus mélange of curtains, ornate wallpaper, chandeliers, sconces, and hand-rubbed hardwoods. In the third, the look is rustic, with a terra-cotta tile floor, brick walls, and a fireplace. The Creole menu is just as varied. Try the oyster trio, oysters Rockefeller accompanied by two other oyster dishes. For another two-taste Creole treat, order the pesto-grilled shrimp Paulina, coated with herb pesto and served with a three-pepper relish.

Crawfish. The identifying authenticity of Louisiana cooking, be it an étouffée or a catfish boil, is crawfish (you must, however, pronounce it as it is spelled: craw-fish, never cray-fish, else you will be the object of much mirth and ridicule). Here are some facts about the critter you should know. They come in handy whether you are ordering or cooking.

Although they were at one time rarely seen over the winter, new production and pond farming techniques have made crawfish quite a common sight in most markets from November through June. Prices are much lower than they used to be, though they are still highest from December to February. It is from late May to October, however, that they reach their full potential in taste. So it is best to delay your boil, or participation in one, until then.

Crawfish are crustaceans that belong to the same family of exoskeletal creatures (that is, the supportive tissue is on the outside) as lobsters and crabs. The shells have posed a problem in their acceptance. Market incentives and technological advances, however, have brought the Louisiana pond crawfish industry to the brink of takeoff as a major farming enterprise.

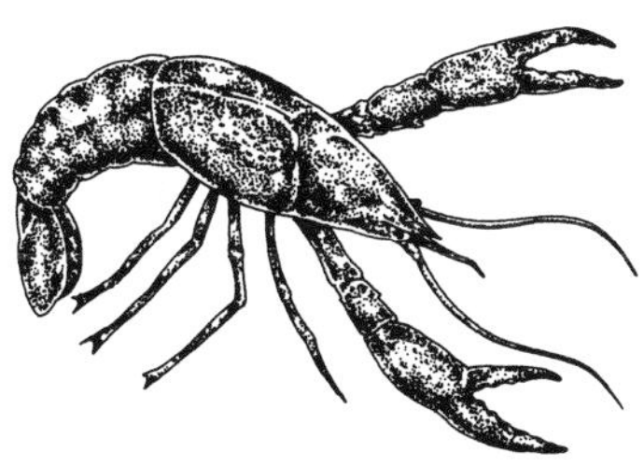

In terms of edible crops under cultivation in the state, the crawfish ranks sixth, behind soybeans, rice, wheat, sugarcane, and grain sorghum. As the market for this almost irresistible delicacy continues to expand, more and more acreage is added for its growth every year.

Although encouraging experiments are underway in Lafayette to produce a soft, edible-shell variety of crawfish, which would greatly enhance its market appeal, existing models still come equipped with shells, which have to be peeled before the meat can be eaten (only the peeled tails are eaten). It takes 10 pounds of crawfish to make 1½ pounds of meat; you need 4 pounds for each person at a crawfish feast.

Crawfish must be boiled before the shells are peeled. The most efficient way to do this is to follow the procedure practiced by commercial operators. The crawfish must remain alive until time for cooking. Wash and inspect your crawfish. Discard debris such as bait and dead crawfish, and wash away mud and dirt from the rest (a common No. 3 washtub serves as a good crawfish washer). Do not add salt to the wash water to "purge" the crawfish. The practice is unnecessary and, in fact, puts the crawfish under stress. After washing them, never place crawfish in airtight containers full of water, or in direct sunlight. Such conditions will quickly kill them—and the object of all this is to keep them alive until you're ready to cook them.

Boiling is the most popular method of cooking crawfish in Louisiana. One way of boiling crawfish is as follows: Bring a pot of water to a rolling boil. The size of the pot will depend on the amount of crawfish you intend to boil. A good rule of thumb is 1 gallon of water for every 2 pounds of the critters. For example, to boil 20 pounds of crawfish you will need at least a 10-gallon pot. Be sure to leave a few inches of clear space at the top of the water level, or the water and foam resulting from the boil will overflow. (If necessary, boil the crawfish in batches.)

Carefully pour the live crawfish into the pot of boiling water—the squeamish should know that crawfish are killed almost on contact with the boiling water. The water stops boiling as the crawfish come into it. Wait until the boiling resumes to begin the timing. Make sure that all the crawfish are submerged in the water. When crawfish are boiled for such dishes as étouffée or bisque, no seasoning is added to the water and the crawfish are boiled for five minutes or less.

For the traditional crawfish boil, or when the crawfish are to be eaten immediately, the cooking water should be well seasoned. Typically, onions, lemon wedges, red pepper, commercial crab-boil seasoning, and salt are added now. As a general rule, add a 1-pound box of salt for each 5 gallons of water. Add other seasonings according to your taste. It is also a Louisiana tradition to boil potatoes, sweet corn (you cut the ear into smaller pieces), and whole onions in the spicy water along with the tiny crustaceans to fill out the meal.

Boil the crawfish for 10 minutes, turn off the heat, and allow them to soak another 10 to 15 minutes before removing them from the water; this allows the crawfish to absorb the flavors of their bath. After the crawfish have been removed from the water, allow them to cool. Now they are ready for peeling. To peel them, do as the Indians did: Select a Peeling Master or appoint yourself. The technique is not hard to learn, demonstrate, or pass on: Place the cooked crawfish—it will be bright red in color—in the palm of the open hand. The tail is what you want to get. Separate the tail and its shell from the head of the animal by slightly twisting and firmly pulling the tail from the head; it should come off where it meets the first joint of the tail. Discard the head. Hold the tail at the sides of the shell, between the thumb and forefinger; then squeeze. Usually you will hear the shell crack along the seams. With your other hand, grasp the larger shell segment from the side and lift up and loosen it from the meat a bit by wiggling it. You will then be able to pull the segmented part of the shell free from the meat and discard it. Firmly grasp the last shell segment, the one with the tail fan, in one hand and the meat with the other hand and gently pull. The last of the meat should slide out of the shell and the vein pull free from the meat. Discard the vein and shell. Congratulations. You have succeeded. The meat of the crawfish tail is now fully peeled and ready for eating, freezing, or adding to your favorite crawfish dish.

If it is not to be eaten immediately, crawfish meat should be packaged in plastic bags, chilled with ice, and stored under refrigeration at a temperature between freezing and 40°F. You can buy and freeze the meat when the critters are plentiful (and cheap) and keep them against those times when they are less plentiful and more expensive. The proper method for freezing crawfish tails is as follows: After peeling, wash all traces of fat from the tails with cold water. If the fat is not removed, it may become rancid in frozen storage, affecting the taste of the meat. There are some who say, however, that it is exactly crawfish fat that imparts the exquisite taste of crawfish to so many things. But why take chances? Your crawfish dealer can supply you with already separated fat, which comes in jars. You use it like butter when the critters are warm, ready to serve.

Just before packaging the cooked tails for freezing, dip them in a weak lemon juice solution. Mix ¼ cup of regular-strength lemon juice with 2½ cups of water to make the solution. Concentrated juice is okay, but reduce it to regular strength for use in the solution. (Attention—too strong a solution will impart a lemony flavor to the meat.) Lemon juice prevents the stored tails from turning "blue." This is a darkening of the meat resulting from freezing. Although harmless, on the plate, blue crawfish tails look unwholesome and unappetizing.

Like most seafood, crawfish are an excellent source of protein. The fat content of washed tail meat is only 2%. Crawfish muscle fibers are shorter than those in red meats and, consequently, more easily digestible. In addition, unlike fish, poultry, or red meats, a peeled crawfish offers no bones to contend with. Crawfish meat is versatile; its delicate, unique flavor comes through whether the meat is eaten alone, fried, or cooked in dishes such as crawfish stew, bisque, or étouffée.

Blue Crab. The waters around New Orleans also constitute one of the great crabbing regions of the world. The critter they catch, and you eat, is the fabulous soft-shell blue crab. The meat of hard-shell crabs can be removed only through a tedious, labor-intensive manipulation called "picking." You are spared this when you eat soft crabs; think of this as you pay for them. They do cost more, but it is my bet you will not regret paying the price as you sit on your bench eating one in Jackson Square.

In Louisiana, soft crabs are not used for commercial meat production at all; only the hard-shell varieties are. Although Louisiana crab meat is usually canned and marketed fresh or frozen, it is sometimes marked "pasteurized." This means that after picking, the crab meat has been sealed and heated to a temperature that kills active microorganisms. The advantage of pasteurized crab meat is a longer shelf life. Properly refrigerated meat handled this way will keep its quality for several months. Without pasteurization, even canned crab meat will keep its quality for only several days.

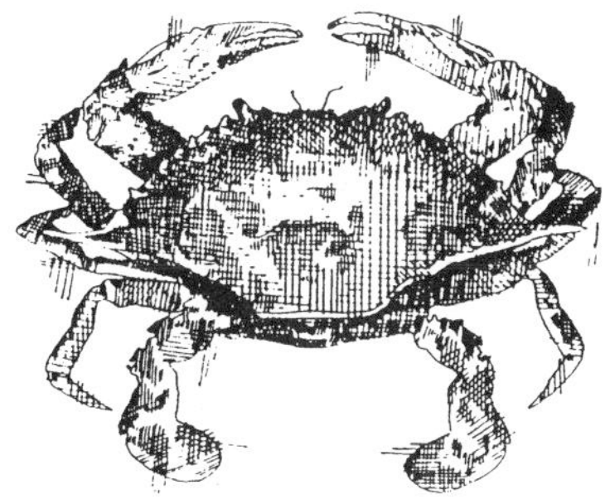

The plentiful clouds of shrimp along the Louisiana coast attract feeding fish in close to the shallows. Others arrive on the Mississippi's flood.

Catfish. Of course, there are the catfish: channel cat, blue cat, and bullhead. All are important food fish—the blue cat is the largest (20–40 pounds); the well-known channel cat, seldom exceeding 25 pounds, has white flesh that is flakier, firmer, and better in flavor than any other cat; the bullhead, found everywhere, but rarely weighing above 5 pounds, makes an excellent pan fish.

Dolphin. Don't worry, we are speaking of the fish here, not the mammal (Flipper). Ram-headed, it can grow to 20 pounds. It is very bright blue, almost neon, flopping into the boat. Apparently, only sportfishing boat captains know how to cook it; it must be grilled on the dock. There is no other way, perhaps because no taste is equal to one smacking of its environment. Once it is cooked, its skin comes off in one leathery strip.

Red snapper and gray snapper. These inhabit the Gulf and swim in schools so dense that the water sometimes takes on the hue of their scales. More than 10 million pounds of this excellent food fish are caught annually in the Gulf of Mexico. Packed in ice, they are shipped throughout the United States, but none will equal the freshness of what you eat here.

Redfish. We decided to bail out and not recommend eating this one because it has been overfished, strenuous limits have been set, and domestically caught redfish have become rare. (*See* Chapter 9, K-Paul's Louisiana Kitchen).

Spadefish. A relative of the angelfish, it weighs as much as 20 pounds. Its color ranges from white to black to black-and-white stripes. Its silvery and savory flesh, esteemed for its delicate flavor, makes it much prized as a food fish. It is usually filleted and sautéed.

Sturgeon. Three types are found in Louisiana, so the state has its own caviar, which is just finding its markets. As for the bony fish itself, leave it to the epicureans; it does not seem to be much used as food.

There are other fishes in these waters we could mention, notably flounder and yellowtail, but we are anxious to get to the fish without the taste of which no food explorer should leave Louisiana.

Pompano. The epicurean favorite—as an early book on American game, *American Wild Life,* once claimed, "the finest food fish of river or ocean," this very silvery 1½-foot-long delicacy is a bottom feeder, dining on shrimp and shellfish, which doubtless greatly contribute to its delectability (too bad for the pompano). It has almost no teeth to defend itself, so tasting as

it does, other fish eat it. Very rarely taken on hook and line, it must be netted. It brings a high price in the market.

There is another finned creature, however, that for its size, curiosity, and presence must be mentioned. Who knows, you might run across one.

Garfish. The alligator garfish is the giant fish of the Mississippi. Ten to 12 feet long, with teeth-filled crocodilian jaws, the alligator gar is a throwback to the dark and distant time when the huge dinosaurs that roamed the land and their contemporaries—the armored, plated, and boneless monsters of the deep—were just giving way to the more agile bony fishes of today. The gar's heavy scales are often found among fossils of extinct forms of life. The first Europeans who came to New Orleans could not believe their eyes: The garfish was the nearest nature had come to an alligator with gills, and it also has a pair of lungs. Serious studies of American wildlife report that the plates of its skin are so tough it cannot be pierced even with an axe. The Cajuns' name for it is *le poisson armé,* and Indians have used its scales for arrowheads. Many bass have been exterminated by gar; the gar will snap off a hook in its jaws unless it can be induced to swallow the bait whole. Indeed, very few fishermen will take one of these thrashing and snapping monsters into a boat. Even unprovoked, the gar has been known to attack humans. A few of the fish are killed, however, each year, by cutting their throat, or with a well-aimed stroke to a vulnerable spot on the back of the head (imagine the struggle). Their flesh has long been relished by Indians and Cajuns. If you think you have a taste for prehistory, you can enjoy it too; in May go to Cajun country for the Garfish Festival.

NEW ORLEANS FOOD ORIGINS

Civilization, even a food culture, doesn't grow on seawater alone. Originally, 12,000 to 9,000 years ago, nomadic families living in the caves of old Mexico collected wild plants and snared small animals and birds. Then, a dramatic shift took place; the people turned increasingly to plants for food. By 8,700 to 7,000 years ago, the people were relying on wild varieties of chili peppers and beans.

Fossil remains in the caves indicate that by about 7,200 years ago wild corn appeared. At first, each ear was no larger than a thumbnail and the whole plant was probably no more conspicuous than many kinds of weeds that grow today in fields and along the roadside. With cultivation, however, corn grew and evolved into the plant with long rows of fat seeds on large cobs.

By 5,400 years ago, the cave dwellers were relying more and more on agriculture, and nearly a third of their sustenance came from crops. The groundwork for civilization was established, and the first permanent settlements appeared in the Americas. By 2,000 years ago the people had developed large-scale irrigation works, domesticated turkeys, and added tomatoes and peanuts to the lengthening list of domesticated plants, which included squash and avocados. They established religion, art, and governments (see what we owe to food?), as well as a far-flung trade. The native cave civilization culminated about 1,000 years ago in the high culture of the Mixtec, who

ruled until they were conquered by the Aztecs shortly before the arrival of Cortés in 1521.

The Native Americans in the vicinity of New Orleans were cultivating corn and other crops and using sophisticated methods of food gathering and preparation when the Europeans arrived. Even the months of the tribal calendar were named for the time edible plants and animals came into season: corn, strawberries, deer, and so on.

Native Americans adapted to many kinds of environments in which they exploited surplus foods as they became seasonally available, without depending on any one particular species. By the time European explorers had reached the center of the country, they discovered that the peoples living in the forests were using 130 plants in their diet. How many plants do you acquire in an excursion to the supermarket? If the answer is five or six, the forest appears to be a better market. The Europeans also discovered that the native people singled out no one animal or group of animals as food sources.

North America was blessed with an environment that could yield a food surplus. It was exactly this surplus that gave rise to the chiefdoms of the Southeast and Northwest. Chiefdoms historically develop in areas where an abundance of food can be obtained from a variety of sources—such as the sea, beaches, forests, rivers, and mountains. In tribes with other types of governments, a band exploits its environment by moving around, going from place to place—first fishing the river, then going into the forest to pick berries, then moving up the slopes to hunt game. A chiefdom can use natural resources much more efficiently, as the people do not move around so much. One band lives near the river, and it fishes; another lives in the forest and hunts; a third gathers plants in the fields. Each band channels the food to a central authority—the chief—who then distributes it to all. The chief is the tribe's economist. It is up to him to see to the laying away of sufficient supplies of food and raw materials for distribution as needed.

Such arrangements led to food surpluses and a technology of food preservation. These developed in the chiefdoms of the northwest coast and the edge of the Caribbean (what is now the southeastern states from Virginia to Texas, plus Central America south of Guatemala, and the large islands of the West Indies and Venezuela). One of the preserved foods the Indians developed was pemmican, a concentrated, highly nutritious substance created for hunters, who sometimes had to move at a moment's notice and often had to eat on the run. The base is corn, parched over the fire to get the water out; the protein comes from lean meat; the fat is from the meat, melted; and carbohydrates are included in the form of wild berries: huckleberries, blackberries, or blueberries, or all three. The berries added taste, and their acid acted as a preservative. The ingredients were dried out separately, then mixed together with the others and pounded and pounded flat again. The mixture was then formed into cakes. Stored in airtight leather bags (frequently mammal bladders), the cakes could stay fresh for up to a few weeks.

The rivers that flowed by the village or camp provided a wealth of food year-round: fishes, turtles, snails, and mussels. It is telling that more than half the fish bones found in the oldest levels of early cave Indian dwellings were those of the catfish, the slower-moving inhabitants of quiet river backwaters.

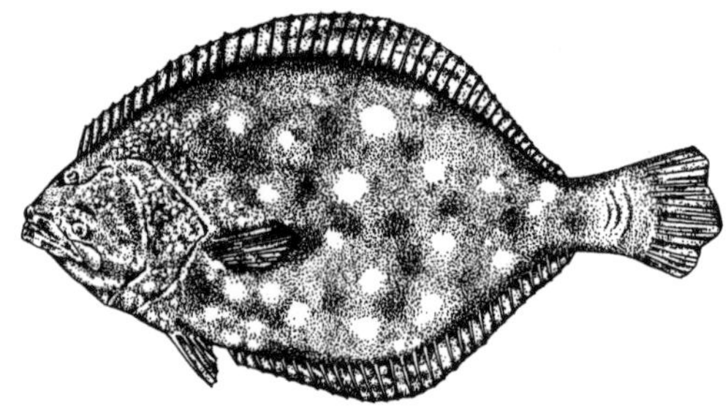

The technology of the earliest peoples was not sufficiently advanced to catch faster-moving fish. That came in time. Where fish were abundant, technology followed—nets, traps, weirs (tidal fish corrals), and other devices were developed.

Salmon were dried, smoked, and even pressed into bales. As several species of fish returned from the ocean to the rivers at different times of year, the Indians could count on five to seven fresh fish runs from spring to fall. In spring came the shad and candlefish, so rich in oil. Cod and halibut swarmed in incredible numbers offshore, and smelt sparkled in the breaking surf. From this bounty the Indians learned to dry and smoke fish and save their protein for lean times, and the New World forms of these arts they taught to the explorers and colonists.

The Mississippi River also had an important role in the formation and perpetuation of the food culture; its churning flood led people to come; then the current made them stay—if you came down in a flat boat, you had to walk back. When the earliest French explorer, René-Robert Cavalier Sieur de la Salle, came floating down the Mississippi and in 1682 claimed the land drained by the river's serpentine coils for the French king, he found a fabulous larder upon which could be based a whole cuisine: trout, red snapper, mullet, flounder, shrimp, crabs, crawfish, and most especially, pompano. To these were added a list of plants, the essences of

which they had never tasted before: sassafras, chicory, and red bay. A whole culture could grow up and survive on these. What has been done with them is the story of New Orleans food today.

It would be easy to say, as some have, that La Salle and the Frenchmen who followed him, coming from a rich culinary tradition, gathered up those things they found and whipped them into the credible cuisine that has been pleasing world palates for 200 years. But such a conclusion is not only incorrect, it ignores the very existence of the original inhabitants. The Choctaw and Chickasaw were more vital than any other group to the development of New Orleans food: They found the explorers, showed them what was edible, and fed them. Without Indian help, European development would not have taken hold—the settlers would have starved.

According to the journal of Penicaute, a ship's carpenter with the expedition, La Salle and the two French Québec-born brothers who followed him, Sieur d'Iberville and Sieur de Bienville, went to live among the Indians, "dined sumptuously on buffalo, bear, geese, ducks, corn, and fruits in all seasons." Later, in the 18th century, the Acadians (Cajuns) came, bringing their single-pot cooking style based on roux (the flour and butter paste used to start the sauce) that was the foundation of their cuisine. New Orleans cuisine was, at first, a democratic

glory, a from-the-ground-up phenomenon, created by the people who enjoyed it.

The first European settlers who came to America were mostly peasants, convicts, and criminals and were unaccustomed to gourmet food. A gruel of boiled, weevil-laden flour, mixed with blood (if they were lucky), carrots, and turnips coated with earth was their staff of life. Bread was the cake of the poor; and of fresh meat and fish they had none. Nor did they know much of cooking *à la bec fin.*

The Ursuline sisters knew. They were among the first Europeans of more sophisticated family and taste to come to Louisiana. They found the local diet, so different from what they had known in Europe, worthy of remark. One sister wrote, in a letter to her family, with telling enthusiasm: "We eat wild beef [probably bison], deer, swans, geese, wild turkeys, rabbits, chickens, ducks, pheasants, partridges, quail and other fowl and game of different kinds. The rivers are teeming with enormous fish unknown in France." She might also have mentioned the shrimp and the oysters—known but seldom seen in France. The missive, and probably others like it, hit home. To the early settlers it was worth the ocean voyage—often in steerage—to taste such delicacies.

In fields not far away, Native Americans were making dazzling progress in a food cultivation that would far outstrip

their discovery of powdered sassafras leaves to thicken a fish soup that was to become known as filé gumbo. When these Indians gave corn to the European settlers, they established the viability of the settlers' community, for corn could be ground and used to prepare bread, cake, and crepes. Also, it could be stored. It would do as a substitute for wheat, which could not be grown around New Orleans because the ground was too wet.

The Indians came up with a way to squeeze out the deadly poison from manioc root, leaving just the white starch, known as tapioca. They also developed the white potato, the sweet potato, tomatoes (first cultivated in America), and peanuts. After rice, corn and the white potato are the foods grown in the largest amounts, by weight, around the world today, outranking even wheat. We will taste these foods in the course of our journey, as many have survived in savory New Orleans and spicy Cajun fare.

Once they caught on, the Europeans didn't do badly at all; they brought back to New Orleans new versions of many of the Indian vegetables and fruits that they had discovered elsewhere in the New World: tomatoes, yams, some squash, and sweet potatoes. What New Orleanians did with them in the kitchen fostered the New Orleans food tradition. The foods were handled and largely cultivated by the Creole (white and black) population, and the word Creole became shorthand

through the rest of America for food excellence. A Creole tomato was bigger and better, Creole strawberries sweeter and bigger, Creole corn tastier and meatier. By the beginning of this century, Creole had come to mean any superior, native-grown farm product. As time passed, new immigrants found new ways of dealing with these crops. The Spanish took the tomato and added it to the roux, coming up with shrimp Creole. Africans created meatless gumbo z'herbes for Lent. Italians turned their fondness for rich red sauces with garlic and bread crumbs into dishes such as stuffed artichokes and eggplant.

Now that we have considered the beginnings of the New Orleans food culture, let us take a dip into how Creole cooking evolved and what it is now.

THE CREOLES

"Creole" is a term misunderstood, mostly by food aficionados and anthropologists. It is not interchangeable with "Cajun." That some restaurants advertise themselves as Creole-Cajun is something that does not clarify the situation, either. Creole is formally defined as "a native of Spanish America, Louisiana, or the West Indies descended from European (originally Spanish) ancestors." It comes from the Spanish *criollo,* meaning born in the colonies, a child of either Spanish, French, West Indian, or African parents. When applied to cuisine, it can mean the same thing—native born but with foreign antecedents. New Orleans was clearly created a French colony and settlement, but in the ebb and flow of wars and politics in Europe it found itself governed by Spain, which influenced its growth for a time. When Spain ceded the colony back to France, French influence rapidly overtook the Spanish, never to be eliminated from New Orleans again, even when the French sold it to the Americans as part of the Louisiana Purchase.

The French settlers, including the Acadians from Nova Scotia, who came to New Orleans came to stay; they brought their families with them. The French language and culture survived, particularly in the bayous. Spanish objectives were different and largely inherited from and following in the wake of the conquistadors. The Spanish adventurer came to make a killing and then go back to Spain to settle down and live like a king. When he didn't, he married a local Creole woman, who brought up their children in the French language and customs with which she was raised.

The Spanish influence was slow to recede from New Orleans; it even strengthened under French rule. Many of the numerous Spaniards who came to New Orleans in this period had been around the New World. Some were seasoned campaigners, had been conquistadors, adventurers, and gourmets. They had been to Mexico and Peru and had tasted the food of the Aztec, Inca, and Mayan cultures. They brought seasonings from out of the bag of tricks of these sources: the red pepper, beans, and yams. Squash, paella, and tacos, too, came with them, and flour ground from corn; mixed with lard or butter the latter became the porridge today called grits in the South.

First brought to Europe (where it was largely ignored) by Christopher Columbus, the tomato was reintroduced into New Orleans by the Spanish. When coupled with roux, it became an integral part of shrimp Creole and Spanish paella. The Spaniards cooked native New Orleans shrimp in enticing new ways. They added it to gumbos, butterflied it, and deep-fried it. They cooked oysters with bacon en brochette.

Curiously, French culture hung on and claimed even these new developments with French names given a new twist: ham, *jambon* in French, added to paella became jambalaya. That made it Creole.

But what did the Creoles themselves become, steeping in the rich cultural sauce of New Orleans? Their culture was so dominant that, after the Purchase, Louisiana became known as "The Creole State." Creole today means culturally very French, espousing the sort of French philosophy that Anglo-Americans and British never understood. "Life is for the living," goes the Creole saying. "If more of us knew how to live, there'd be fewer of us dead."

For the New Orleans Creole, a major part of living had to do with food: "Garden far off, gumbo is ruined," they also said. Wherever they moved, they had gardens, close by the back door to their kitchen, and tended them mercilessly—on all fours, picking off aphids from the tomato leaves and

mealy bugs from the potato plants. As for the snails, they ate them.

This all paid off in the larger-than-life produce that they succeeded in raising and in using to create their étouffées, gumbos, and jambalayas. As for garlic, Creoles espoused the French directive: "Even the chef should be rubbed with it." The Creoles like to give you something to think about with their food. That's why there are two tastes in one dish: The two components are very similar in structure and form, but have contrasting tastes—like oysters and foie gras. To keep the mouth guessing is the object of much of their cuisine; the Creoles like to play with tastes. They like to play. This must be understood. Even a masterpiece is capable of arousing a laugh.

The New Orleans Creoles found that the flavors of the foods available to them—anything from old raccoon meat to "mudbugs" (crawfish)—were made all the more palatable with hot spices and red peppers. If the hot pepper influence in New Orleans was ever in danger, the fire was intensified when thousands of Louisiana boys went off to fight the war with Mexico and returned home with their pockets bulging with new and exotic sorts of peppers. One returning veteran of the wars brought the McIlhenny family of Avery Island some special and redoubtable pepper seeds. The result was Tabasco sauce. Gobbling hot peppers (especially of the pickled variety)

remains a highly competitive sport in southern Louisiana barrooms. Enter one and you may be challenged. The antidote for pepper burn, by the way, is to swallow not water, but milk.

In classical French cuisine, equal parts of butter and flour are blended together over heat to create a base (roux; from the French *roux beurre,* rusty butter) that will be the tasting agent of the dish to come, created on top of it. The Creoles did not throw this out but married it to what was available, raising the taste of roux to a dimension never before achieved in classical cooking. Lard, peanut oil, bacon fat, and eventually duck fat were substituted for butter and used in combination with the flour to produce many variations in taste and color undreamed of in France.

Another thing to remember about Creole dining is that it is a leisurely pastime. No one rushes through a meal in New Orleans. People congregate around a dinner table here like game in Africa around a water hole. Observe them; no one is in a hurry to get through eating. Dinner is a place to hold a conversation, and no one is in a hurry to end it. The meat hovers on its fork. The mouth moves; the words flow.

Creole Nouvelle Orléans remained basically a French city for almost 100 years after the Louisiana Purchase. When the English-speaking Anglo-Americans arrived in great numbers after 1803, the Creoles considered *les Américains* for-

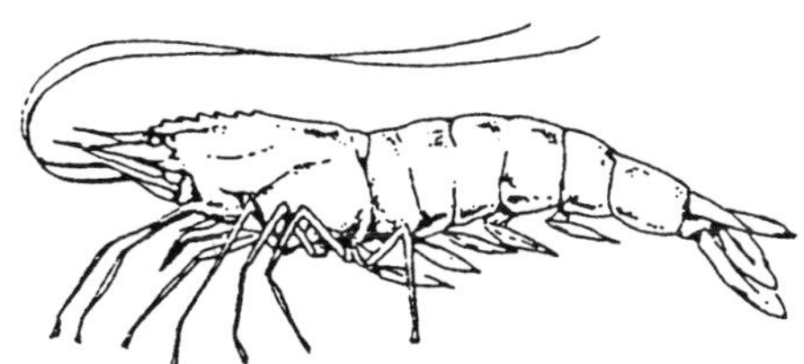

eign interlopers who would ruin a good thing, and they stubbornly clung to their lifestyle and language in the face of overwhelming numbers and change. By the end of the last century, old New Orleans had become synonymous with a way of life and an atmosphere unknown elsewhere in the United States—and a cuisine as well. Throughout this century, the city represented an island of blissful detachment from the frantic society rapidly growing into today's machine-made world.

Of the many recipes the Creoles have handed down to their offspring, one seems the most valuable, and confounding: Relax, enjoy this delicious inheritance we have left you. Remember never to rush the sauce, but let it simmer of its own accord a long time. You will see; it will come out all right—in the end.

THE BASIS OF CREOLE

In classical French cuisine, a brown roux was used for brown sauces; a blond roux for veloutés, and white roux for béchamels. In Creole cuisine a brown roux (from bacon fat) is used to thicken gumbos and stews where a lightness of taste is desired. Certain gumbos are further thickened with okra or filé powder.

Cooks at home should remember, however, what the Creoles discovered: The thickening properties of the dark roux are diminished due to the fact that the darker the roux gets, the more the starch compound—which thickens the liquid—breaks down. Butter, therefore, is used in classical (as in French) Creole roux.

In the Creoles' adaptation of their lifestyles to their new environment, the principles of stocks were essential. Whether in a hunter sauce for a loin of venison or to braise a rabbit *à la sauce piquante,* the stock makes the difference, as the Creoles know. Old World principles were adapted with local ingredients to produce a cuisine that was truly American.

Even in America, stocks have four main ingredients, as observed by the Creoles:

Bones. Any bones available in the kitchen may be used. For white stocks—veal, fish, or chicken—wash any blood off the bones and cut them up into manageable size for the pot, exposing any marrow. For dark stocks—game or duck—brown the bones well. A light coating of oil dribbled over them may help. Well-browned bones add rich color and flavor, but burning or charring them will make the stock bitter.

Mirepoix. A mixture of aromatic vegetables—onions, shallots, scallions, leeks, celery, mushroom trimmings, and tomatoes—will infuse flavor into the stock. For brown stocks, these can be added to the bones as they brown. For white stocks, the mirepoix can be slightly sweetened by sautéing them in butter.

Bouquet garni. Black peppercorns, parsley, whole thyme, bay leaf, and cloves—tied up in either a leek or cheesecloth—are placed in the liquid.

Liquid. The purpose of stock is to extract the color, flavor, nutrients, and gelatin from the bones. Cold water is the first medium for this process. It can be supplemented by either red or white wine. Cold liquid is the best agent to draw the flavor out of bones. Start, therefore, with cold water, bring the

bones to a boil, and lower the heat. Long cooking time draws out the flavor. *Never* add salt to the water in making a stock. The salt will remain as the liquid volume reduces, and you will be stuck with a salty stock. Creoles simmer stocks very slowly, skimming off all impurities and fat that rise to the surface, producing the hearty and flavorful clear stock demanded in so many of their recipes.

No early Creole home was without the aroma of a constantly simmering stockpot filled with bones, shellfish, or game, into which the roux, together with onions, shallots, and vegetables, was stirred to make a rich sauce always at the ready for anything—especially the demands of little Creole boys and girls running home from school. This rich sauce dolloped on toasted French bread was turned over to eager reaching hands. This was lunch; the onion, butter, and vegetables were as sweet as any chocolate, the bread soaked and crunchy, and quickly gobbled up. Is it any wonder that generations of food lovers were to come from this background, and that they furthered and propagated the most interesting cuisine in America?

CREOLE CLASSICS

Here are some Creole specialties that you'll find on New Orleans tables:

Gumbo. The name for this soup comes from the West African word for okra. African-Americans (born in this country, usually with one French Creole parent) were great in number among Creoles and were known as Creoles of color. They had a strong impact on New Orleans music and food. Africans brought over to Louisiana on slave ships carried with them okra seeds. The New Orleans diet was to be the chief beneficiary of this culinary farsightedness. Now this vegetable is used to flavor any number of the dark, stewlike soups called gumbos. Frequent other ingredients in a gumbo are shrimp, oysters, crab, chicken, andouille sausage, duck, and turkey. The gumbo is usually, but not always, served over white rice.

Jambalaya. Rice is the recognizable ingredient in this Creole offshoot of Spanish paella; ham is also in it. There is also usually some shrimp, sausage, green pepper, and celery cooked in a thick tomato sauce rich with spices. The flavor should be strong, with nothing laid-back about it. To taste these two staples of New Orleans dining you should go to places where they are most accessible and popular with the tastes of the people.

THE GUMBO SHOP

630 St. Peter St. (French Quarter)
Tel. 504/525-1486

Small and quaint, it's easy on the eyes, with its old murals (of Jackson Square in early days). It has easy, friendly service; the waitresses make you feel at home. It's also easy on the pocketbook—the gumbo (take the chicken and andouille) is only $5.95 a bowl. There is very good red beans and rice, another New Orleans staple, at an equal bargain price, and everything is served with a smile and loaves of very hot French bread. The gumbo is why most people come to the shop, though. It's made from a dark roux (this can be had, even Creole style, by cooking the flour in the butter longer, until it's mahogany—instead of peanut-butter—color); there are big pieces of chicken dredged up from the murky depths with the spoon, along with pink-color rounds, cross sections of sausage, and everything has a deep-down taste without being salty. The flavor is complex, with a sweet undertaste from the stock, and is perfect for dipping bread. For dessert there is a special New Orleans treat that you must come here to get: Praline Sundae. The secret to the intriguing taste (the New Orleanians have a way with pralines like no one else) is that the sauce is almost burned. It comes up with a sweetness different from what you'll find most anywhere else. After you pass a very enjoyable hour on the clock, you can step out onto St. Peter Street without having used more than a $10 bill.

Happy surprises like these, thrown in the path of our budget, can extend our stay. After doing the proper intelligence work (asking around is always necessary on food explorations), we look forward to some upscale Creole treats.

THE TOUCH OF CLASSIC

Of the great New Orleans restaurants in the following group, most are exceptionally well known. With anticipation and appetite then, we dive into them with no preparation other than our great expectations. Try to go to a restaurant first with a native; read a book with a good glossary on New Orleans cuisine, so that you'll know what to order or, at least, what is proposed. Entering one of the grand New Orleans restaurants, you are in the eye of a food culture second to none in the world, where the waiters are members of an old, professional caste system, with a long and honorable tradition. They take the demystification of a menu and the comfort of a client as both a pleasure and a professional duty.

ARNAUD'S

813 Bienville St. (French Quarter)
Tel. 504/523–5433

After we have tested the waters with beignets and a Creole hangout, Arnaud's is the proper mirror to hold up for New Orleans food reflections. Arnaud's, founded in 1918, is a place not only for classic Creole cuisine, but for the time traveler. Entering the restaurant, we cross the threshold not of the cutting edge of cuisine, but of a traditional French restaurant of the Empire stamp. The waiters wear black ties, mosaic tiles checker the floors, ceiling fans turn unhurriedly, and 10 multibulb chandeliers dip from a ceiling held up by graceful columns fluted like champagne glasses. This is old, classical France; if you don't have the money (or a space warp vehicle) to visit there, spend your money here. The staff is expert and the service a joy. It is just like being in France except that the air-conditioning works. (In New Orleans this is indispensable, and it keeps up the appetite.)

We are shown to a corner table and I ask for a Chardonnay, one with some size, but not an oaky one, or tasting of lemon, and it is just that. I settle into a bentwood chair and enjoy the offering from Royce vineyards, a very good house wine indeed. I am with a New Orleanian and, with the

waiter's guidance (a violation of Halliday's Rules—never trust the maître d'hôtel—it is true, but Tony is very professional), we zero in on my order, marrying it to the specialties of Arnaud's.

The restaurant is famous for shrimp Arnaud. Shrimp in a rémoulade sauce, it comes as a creamy, brick-color blend of Creole mustard, paprika, oil, vinegar, chopped vegetables, and other seasonings (but hold the mayo). The palate, awakened and craving more shrimp, doesn't get it; for, in a coup of food psychology, what immediately next passes beneath our noses is a bowl of turtle soup. If you've heard of it only in literature and thought turtle soup existed in food fable, the dish itself is a food lover's awakening, and worth the trip to New Orleans

(where turtles are ranched just for soup) to taste it. Arnaud's is intensely green, as the tree-tops of a piney forest, and spicy. Bouillon-based—another surprise—it is loaded with meat. Thick and tart, it is almost a meal in itself. We go very slowly, consuming with the rich liquid an original dip: Arnaud's *pommes de terre soufflés* (potato puffs). Everybody does these a little differently; these are long and tapering, like lady fingers, and tasting of potatoes, with a sprinkle of salt.

For the main course, we try a house specialty called veal Wohl, which is crabmeat and crawfish centered on medallions of sautéed veal. By now you understand. Like New Orleans itself, Arnaud's is no place for the gastronome of faint heart. You will be fed. Each bite of this unique veal Wohl offers a taste harmony on a different level—the salt brine of the crabmeat, the snap of the crawfish tails—each plays with and offsets the other; the delicate squish of the veal adds a luxurious touch, and the entire dish is a wonderful and typical Creole food conceit.

To end this festive dinner at Arnaud's, the perfect setting for the dramatic, we choose bananas Foster. The dish is concocted at table side: The sliced bananas are placed in their shallow dish and sprinkled with brown sugar; the liquors, Myers's rum and Curaçao, are mixed and poured directly onto the brown sugar. The plate is flambéed with a sudden, blue whoosh! The taste is excellent, but wait 'til the fire is out. The alcohol burns away, and what is left is the soft sweetness of the fruit and crunchy caramel. We walk away with the most satisfying of tastes in our mouths; Arnaud's is a temple of substantial elegance.

From dinner at a place where hunger is unknown we proceed for our next meal to a place where it is banned: breakfast at Brennan's.

Brennan's

417 Royal St. (French Quarter)
Tel. 504/525–9711

Breakfast? A new word must be invented for it, and it cannot be brunch (also invented at Brennan's), for brunch is only a combination of breakfast and lunch. Breakfast at Brennan's is a combination of things you probably never had for lunch either.

Breaded crawfish (deep-fried), oysters Rockefeller, bananas Foster—it's hard to believe we will have these sump-

tuous sweets again, or that we could pass them up; strawberries Fitzgerald (a sort of bananas Foster but with strawberries), Creole onion soup, eggs Hussarde, eggs Benedict, turtle soup (we're anxious to try it again). Who has ever breakfasted like this? Maybe Louis XVI, maybe Catherine the Great. The setting of the feast is just as delicious: a tropic garden set like a wet emerald in a classic atrium frame. The mood is exotic; you dine among palm fronds, spiraling fuchsia, hibiscus, and ferns, with a ceiling open to the sky. For an eye-opener, there's a brandy milk punch (half-and-half, brandy, and nutmeg in a large frosted glass).

We start with three eggs: Benedict, Sardou, and Hussarde, served on the same plate, for comparison. Benedict:

poached, atop Holland rusks, with Canadian bacon, and topped with hollandaise sauce. The Sardou eggs are poached on artichoke bottoms, nestled in a bed of creamed spinach and covered with hollandaise. The taste is there, and the Gewürztraminer (served with it) is generously poured. Eggs Hussarde are a variation on eggs Benedict, with the addition of *marchand de vin* (meat and red wine) sauce.

Then we pass on to three soups: oyster, Creole onion, and turtle. The oyster soup is light green, subtle, and superb in orchestrated harmonies of oyster taste that range from clear to rich. The Creole onion is mahogany in color, thick and syrupy. Brennan's turtle soup is red in color, spicy, and meaty. It is so delicious and filling that the waiter cautions us to save room for what is to come: oysters Rockefeller. Here is another version of the dish—six on their half shells; these are very meaty and in Brennan's special sauce, with anise cream.

This is breakfast—as ordered—but you can have a taste of almost anything else from the menu. The waiters and chef parade up and down, offering complimentary smidgens of this, and tastes of that; be sure to snag the *grillades* (small pieces of grilled meat) and grits. The mood is generous, free, and easy. With regret, but no need for lunch, we depart.

Breakfast at Brennan's has put an edge on our appetite for a unity of beauty and food. At the end of this day we come to the most romantic setting for dining in all New Orleans.

The Court of Two Sisters

613 Royal St. (French Quarter)
Tel. 504/522–7261

This place of meetings and banquets is one of the loveliest in the city. Set in a grove of trees, with trellises overhead dripping flowering plants, it has gaily strung lights that glow softly in the night. The fountain near where I am seated is lighted from the bottom up and seems to shimmer. The murmuring of voices melds with the twitter of birds. This is a place of enchantment. It happens that the food is good, too. What strikes the traveler is that the produce is so good in New Orleans: Crawfish, prawns, pompano—where else can you have such a larder, all fresh, never frozen? I settle on *écrevisses* (crawfish) *étouffées* and on the main dish of the evening, pompano *en papillote* (steamed in a paper bag to keep its juices from escaping). The service is fast, the étouffée generous and delicious—*"ça pique,"* as they say here. The crawfish is tart,

accompanied by minced garlic, green onions, and bell pepper. I drink a Piesporter and am happy.

The pompano comes: at last, this local fish about which I have heard so much but which, until now, has eluded me. It is whole and not the least scale of it looks disturbed. I cut away the paper envelope, and it lies steaming in a bed of its own juices, along with bell pepper, green onion, a little cream, and some shrimp and lobster meat, too. It is a taste with no antecedent. Fish it is, but it comes on almost like chocolate—chunky and sweet, boneless, but with plenty of spine in it—like eating steak with fins. It's too mellow to be meat: the perfect entrée for the vegetarian, as well as for someone who does not want to be one. All by itself, this one experience is worth the trip to New Orleans.

Sitting back, finishing the wine, and looking at the animated Degas portraiture wrapped around me, I reflect that what I like most about The Court of Two Sisters is that it is not overworked or overdone. There is an ease and simplicity of style that comes through all. The formula is good food, simply prepared, but with high palate interest. And there is this final touch—personal service. The table sweeper comes up and asks, "Can I offer you a cappuccino? Espresso? Or what would you like?" Very interesting, and revealing. Most restaurants never let their table cleaners offer anything; it isn't up to them. But in the relaxed New Orleans food culture they do things differently; the object is to serve. There is a pride in this and a professionalism that is unexcelled elsewhere. A further plus here is the daily jazz brunch—the only one in the city.

Pleasingly sated, we have tasted the Creole New Orleans restaurant scene. It is a place of stunning, sophisticated city taste: near mismatches, haphazard harmonies, Euro-American alliances, and happenstance deftly tossed in the air and falling on the palate in a symphony of incredible richness. Now we can go on to taste Creole in its 19th-century form.

A TALE OF THREE HOUSES

Right in the heart of New Orleans there exist three hearths simmering with the Creole secrets of ways of living and cuisine as practiced by these people and passed on to this city and to us. You have only to take your place and be seated to see and taste how it is done.

HERMANN-GRIMA HOUSE

820 St. Louis St. (French Quarter)
Tel. 504/525–5661

The handsome, three-story, brick Federal home is a National Historic Landmark, and it is accredited by the American Association of Museums, but that is only one reason to come here. The others involve the completeness of the house as a pre–Civil War Creole family living quarters, the flower-planted courtyard, the slave quarters, and a look inside its kitchen at the preparation of food and meals.

We enter under the fan window above the cypress entrance door. The long dining-room table with its white cloth is set as for dinner for eight, but the guests today are shown into the cozy working kitchen, for Creole cooking is our main interest. We assemble eagerly within the mellow, stuccoed walls for a live demonstration of Creole cooking around and inside the massive fireplace. From the Colonial period to the Civil War there were few indoor stoves, because of the smoke and fire hazard, so this is where meals were cooked. The kitchen is large, and set out on its shelves and crannies are many vessels of wood, pottery, copper, and ironwork that cry out to be touched and felt. The fireplace opening is about 3½ feet wide, and the chimney stained with smoke. Its fire walls are equipped with all the right ironwork impedimenta for cooking: movable cranes, a fixed *crémaillère* (toothed rack) riveted into the brick, from which are suspended iron pots that you'd be certain to have if only you had such a fireplace to begin with. The wooden oak table and bowls set before the fireplace are appropriately yellowed and mellowed with the glowing patina of age. The logs are set on the andirons, and the kindling underneath is ignited. One of the cooking team of two women explains why she is doing this now: One of the dishes to be made today is a gumbo; they will fire up the *potager* (a sort of trestle oven with several empty bays for soup bowls, to the left of the fireplace). To the right is a beehive oven (for bread). While the wood is burning, the flame going up the chimney with a big "whoosh!" and, thankfully, the smoke too, the two women repair to the oak table. On it, in bowls and wooden dishes, are most of the ingredients they will be cooking. There are also cutting boards.

The Creole cooking at the Hermann-Grima House embodies the word "Creole." Here are the recipes, realized at this house, that are the essence of Creole. Nobody does recipes like these. Not any restaurant. Not any cookbook anymore. Once you read them, you won't wonder why. To give you a true flavor of the art of Creole cooking, here they are as they were presented and tasted in this house—transcribed directly from the Creole of the 19th century.

First course:

SOUP À L'AURORE

Take some carrots, the reddest that are to be met with, scrape them well; wash them clean; then take off the outside till you come to the middle part. Sweat it in about a quarter of a pound of fresh butter, on a very slow fire. When the carrots are soft enough, put in a crust of bread well rasped, and moistened with some good broth. Let the whole boil for about an hour, and rub it through a tammis [sieve, from French *tamis*], then pour a little more broth in, that it may boil again. Skim it; when you have taken off the fat, it will be of a reddish color. Put in some bits of soft bread cut into dice, that have been fried in butter till they are light brown. Observe that purée is perfection only when the carrots are new, old carrots will not answer: this purée may be used with rice paste, & etc.

—from *The French Cook,* by Eustache Ude, 1841.

Such are the ingredients of what we will taste.

Meat course:

LEG OF MUTTON À LA KRETCHMER

Begin by elevating, with a very sharp knife, the skin which covers the leg, and which forms a sort of parchment; debone it if you have not already had it boned by the butcher; take a half pound of fresh butter or finely hashed lard; put on only a quarter pound if the

leg is small; rub together salt, pepper, parsley, hashed green onions, a pinch of fine flour; make of this a sort of rolled sausage, which you will introduce into the cavity of the mutton in place of the bone. Split this and hold in place with skewers and some thread; having put it on the fire, it is necessary to sprinkle it with salt and pepper, and coat it with bread crumbs in the following manner: coat it liberally with oil, grease or soft butter and roll it in fine bread crumbs, in a way that it holds as much as possible. Sprinkle it again with as much flour as it will hold; put it on the fire and turn it gently. Sprinkle it again with flour while you turn it; it is essential to observe that one does not have to baste this roast as one does others. The bread crumbs, the flour and grease hold together perfectly during the cooking and form the most useful crust, since it prohibits the evaporation of the juices of the meat. When this precious mutton is served and when the knife pierces it, the guests will see, with a completely delectable feeling, torrents of juices will run out and we will understand already that it will be their first recognition for the invention of this delicious dish. Also, let us consider it a duty to offer his [Kretchmer's] name for the admiration of gourmets present and future.

—from *La Petite Cuisinière Habile,* 2nd edition: New Orleans, 1840. Translated by Martha Irwin, volunteer cook at Hermann-Grima Historic House.

The cooks explain every step of their operation as they make the gumbo, while fielding questions from the onlookers. As one cuts up some onion and slices and mashes garlic in a pestle and mortar, the other uses the fireplace crane to edge a black kettle over the flames, just enough to heat the bottom. She knocks down the burning logs and places a grill atop them and then hauls the kettle to the worktable. Then the two women hoist another kettle onto one of the hooks of the crémaillère. The flames are just the right height around it. One cook dribbles a little oil into the warmed pot, and then in goes the cut and crushed garlic. There is a moment's wait, we smell the garlic, and then the cook adds the onions. There isn't even a sizzle; the pot isn't hot enough to do the cooking; it just starts the caramelization (of the onions).

Some books will tell you Creoles used only butter to make roux, but we watch as one of the cooks moves the onion and garlic over to the edge of the pot and into its center spoons about 2 tablespoons of flour, upon which she dribbles down a thin stream of oil. "If you want a thicker, darker gumbo," she says, "use a little oil in your roux, but never, never burn it. If you burn it, and little black specks show up, dump it out and start all over again." With the pot warmed only by the fire, there is no risk of burning the roux. To finish its cooking process, once safely started and with the onion mix to take up some of the heat, the cook places the pot on the grill and continues the stirring.

When the roux is finished, the cook tilts the pot to show the inside and we all lean forward to look; it's a nice, uniform, shiny mahogany brown. Then she slides back the onion-garlic mixture to the center and stirs it into the roux. Meanwhile, the other cook has been boiling a broth in a kettle, and now it steams. A chopped-up bell pepper goes into the onions and roux; the cook stirs the pot more and then pushes it over the grill toward the back, where the flames are more intense, for a few additional moments. Presently it cooks faster, as we can hear. The cook takes it off the heat and puts it on the hearth, and a very appealing aroma fills the kitchen.

There are other dishes to prepare, such as the appetizer. Have you ever heard of corn oysters? Well, they're from an 1885 recipe. One cook mixes milk, a tad of butter, and corn meal and spices into a batter. Then come shelled oysters out of an urn; she dredges them through the batter, deep-fries them in a skillet, and then displays them on a plate. Among the spices was cayenne. Corn seems just the right agent for an oyster crackling; it's textured and gives the oyster a nice, layered taste. The oil is sweet, too, for a gentle aftertaste.

While we are watching, the cooks add the hot broth to the pot with the roux, stir it, and set it on the grill again. They add shrimp and diced vegetables to the broth. The broth, we learn, is shrimp mixed with chicken and has been simmering for about an hour. "What we are trying to achieve here is only a marriage," we are told. As always with gumbo, and Creole cooking, nothing is thrown away; shells are eaten. Marriage achieved, the cooks ladle the gumbo into bowls, which are laid into the potager. They shovel burning charcoal from the fireplace into the burner underneath. The heat goes up the duct, warms the bowls, and then is ventilated out a flue to the outside. Ingenious, these 19th-century builders.

History becomes palpable as we see egg whites whipped with birch whisks, smell gumbo simmering on the potager, feel the intense heat and bustle of a 19th-century kitchen. "We had to rebuild the chimney a few years ago," we are told, "to make it work like it was supposed to. It was very expensive." Restoration began in 1977 and included extensive research, archaeological investigation, and preservation of surviving architectural elements. Original flagstones were replaced on the floor and original paint colors were recreated by a local specialist.

Out of the beehive oven, to go with the gumbo, comes corn bread. It is puffy and hot to the touch. It has a nice chewy texture and is good as a muffin. The rest of the meal comes forth in little chunks of surprises. Macaroni in a mold, held together with cheese. Chicken fricassee Marengo, the Napoleonic favorite: Marengo was one of his important victories, and this dish was its celebration. The recipes are culled from original old-time sources. The chicken Marengo was from *The Virginia Housewife* by Mary Randolf, published in 1824; the corn oysters came out of *La Cuisine Creole* by Lafcadio Hearn, published in 1885.

Finally come a salad and a surprise dessert—frozen peaches and cream. As ice was expensive in New Orleans, using it in the preparation of a showy Creole dinner was obligatory. It helped to make the last impression favorable.

They do all sorts of interesting food-related things at the Hermann-Grima House. In May comes the annual fine wine auction and buffet. Cooking and dinners take place all day Thursday from October through May. Groups touring the house can peek in as the cooking is going on. By special arrangement, you can come for dinner at a cost of $150. It is prepared in the open-hearth kitchen and served in the gallery. They aim to please and will try to cook what you want to taste and learn from. Remember, the cooking appendage of the Hermann-Grima House is an educational institution, and the cooks are trained food historians.

From this 1831 building we step forward to a time and decor only 16 years later, but into a place that exhibits the remarkable 19th-century inventiveness of its famous architect-builder owner. You will get nothing to eat at the following address, but it does have a splendid array of food-related vessels and furnishings.

GALLIER HOUSE MUSEUM

1118–1132 Royal St. (French Quarter)
Tel. 504/523–6722

If you ever wanted to enter the wild, quirky world of Victoriana in a house that was operationally up to snuff, and even opulent, here's your chance. James Gallier, Jr. (his Irish father changed the family name of Gallagher to the more French-sounding and socially acceptable Gallier), who built this house, was one of the city's leading architects in his day. He was responsible for such New Orleans landmarks as the French Opera House, which burned down in 1919; City Hall, today Gallier Hall, a fine example of the Greek Revival style that swept the city—with Gallier's help—and the Bank of

America Building, which is still standing. It was the first building in New Orleans with a structural cast-iron front.

Always interested in innovations, Gallier invested the latest architectural touches and flourishes in his house, including the etched glass skylight (it is operational) above the upstairs landing and ventilators in the ceiling of the master bedroom: Two little holes you can poke open with a poke pole let oppressive New Orleans heat escape and allow you to sleep comfortably. There is also a flush toilet, one of the first in the city. Especially noteworthy, however, after a visit to the Hermann-Grima Creole kitchen, is the Gallier kitchen. No fireplace here: There's a stove. It was not the custom in the 19th century, because of the risk of fire, to have kitchens in the house; you had to walk to them, like privies. Gallier, however, had a different idea; he would bring the kitchen inside, vent the stove perfectly to the outside, and be able to fix his breakfast when it rained without getting his feet wet. The stove itself, rare in America at the time, he was forced to import. It is a 4-foot-long by 4½-foot-high monster—a cast-iron, coal-burning English range made by T. Hudson's Exors of Manchester, with a thick fire wall. That wasn't enough. Gallier had a brick couchlike area built for the stove to sit in. Behind the stove was a reservoir of water, which would be heated by the stove and provide hot water. Behind the reservoir was a cistern to absorb any additional heat. The stove, which had two cast-iron hot plates and an oven, was vented through the waterworks to the outside by a brick-encased pipe. The arrangement was complicated, but it worked.

Gallier installed further custom-made creature comforts so that he never need leave home. Two cisterns—one 2,500 gallons, the other 5,000 gallons—provided water directly to the indoor faucets. Hot water circulated from a copper boiler through the range and then upstairs to the copper bathtub, which the architect greatly enjoyed.

The rest of the museum is meticulously restored according to the descriptions in an 1868 inventory of Gallier's estate.

As rare as the stove, and equally remarkable, is a complete suite of furniture by Prudent Mallard (the singular New Orleans cabinetmaker). He was a Frenchman who came to New Orleans in the 1830s and opened a shop on Royal Street, where his work became much in demand and his services were sought by the gentry of the city. His suite at the Gallier House shows off his painstaking efforts to their best advantage. It consists of a dresser, two armoires (a French specialty), a washstand, a nightstand, and a half-tester (canopy) bed. Aside from its fine workmanship, design, and detail, this furniture is all the more remarkable because it is rare solid rosewood. The wood, from Central America, must have cost a pretty penny.

Also of note is the equally rare and fine full parlor of Belter furniture, upholstered and with rosewood trim. Look closely at this work. John (originally Johann) Belter was a German immigrant who came to New Orleans after landing and working for a time in New York around 1844. His professional story is an illustration, once again, of the critical relationship between commerce and creativity—and of what money can do for the arts. At the time, the Creole city had grown rich on cotton and indigo. Belter had need of the local millionaires for his specialty. The furniture artist specialized in what was called Rococo Revival. He steam-pressed 16 thin sheets of rosewood and laminated them together in such a way as to crisscross their magnificent grains. The rosewood trim on his upholstered pieces—sofas, chair backs, and so on—is layered at a 90-degree angle, an unusual and eye-catching treatment designed to show the grains and tones of this matchless wood to its best possible advantage. Who else but a millionaire planter (or his architect) could pay what it took for this kind of work? The Belter parlor here is a collection of his work as complete as exists anywhere. It consists of a sofa in three sections, a straight-back, long-armed "gentleman's chair," four armless (yes, lady's) side chairs, all exhibiting the layered rosewood treatment, and a meridian chair—a half sofa with a lowered seat. This chair was designed so ladies could recline in hooped skirts without being immodest.

As for more Victorian quirkiness, the house is equipped with goffering irons. Made of iron, weighing as much as 12 pounds and standing in 4-foot-high holsters, these presses were heated on the stove's searing iron plates and used for ironing laces and ruffles. It is great fun to sit with the museum's stereoscope, a two-lensed viewer popular in the late 19th and early 20th century that shows three-dimensional images so real-seeming that you can almost reach out and touch them. The images for this viewer include such popular Victorian subjects as famous buildings and historical scenes.

Worth a look, too, to understand the effects of the subtropical summer heat on the inhabitants of the city and their unusual insect problems, are the parts of the house that are displayed in "summer costume." Straw matting is extensively used to replace wool carpets. Mirrors, chandeliers, and all reflecting objects are covered with mosquito netting, to protect them against the permanent black-spotting of flyspecks. Throughout the house, in summer, the upholstered furniture is draped with white cotton slipcovers that are cooler to the body than the heavy velvets and brocades of traditional Victoriana.

In addition to a summer style of furnishings, a summer style of eating was ushered in during the Lenten season. The Creoles excel in the preparation of soups without meat, or fast-day soups, as they are called. The ingenuity of the cooks from generation to generation has been taxed in the preparation of these soups. But many of them, such as cream of asparagus soup and cream of celery soup, have entered into the daily life of the city, and, like the famous Creole gumbos, are held as dainty and elegant introductions to the most distinguished feasts.

Besides touring the premises, you can also take in short films on architectural crafts that instruct you on the finer points of what to look for here, as well as exhibits of 19th-century life in New Orleans. Special food exhibits are held from time to time. Finally, there is a gift shop. In addition to its apparent charms, the house is said to be haunted by a thoughtful ghost who smells of lavender and lights the fireplaces on chilly mornings. The carriageway outside is one of the few in the city not choked with cars. A carriage—itself an object of admiration—is actually parked in it.

Also worthwhile to see, because of its singular garden and its most whimsical and exclusive tea party, is the Beauregard-Keyes House, which stands in the French Quarter across the street from the Ursuline Convent. The convent, which dates from 1734, is the oldest French colonial building in the Mississippi Valley and is itself worth a look. It was the site of the oldest girls' school—the Ursuline Academy, founded in 1727—in the country.

BEAUREGARD-KEYES HOUSE

1113 Chartres St. (French Quarter)
Tel. 504/523–7257

In all seasons, this fine mansion has one of the loveliest gardens you ever will see. Alive and thriving with new blooms all year, plantings around the stately center oak show off pink ruffled azaleas, big green sprays of fern, and trumpets of Louisiana peppermint camellias. Especially note the French parterre, with a meandering path that circulates through year-round ornamental beds, bringing you as close as possible to the white magnolias and petunias, as well as the herb garden. The house was once the residence of the Southern hero and Confederate General P. G. T. Beauregard. Dating from 1826, it is the last Greek Revival raised cottage remaining, except for Tezcuco Plantation (*see* Chapter 8) on the Great River Road. The style was very popular in and around New Orleans in the early part of the 19th century.

It was General Beauregard's command that authorized the first shots fired on Fort Sumter. It could be said that Pierre Gustave Toutant Beauregard started the Civil War. At the dawn of the war, he was a great hero in the South. Things change: After the war, he was accused of collaborating with the Union army during Reconstruction. When he accepted an ambassadorship from Ulysses S. Grant and left New Orleans and the country, there was nobody left to protect his reputation or his property. His house fell into ruin.

The novelist Frances Parkinson Keyes brought it back, investing much of the money gained from her writing in it. Her studio at the back of the large courtyard is where she wrote 40 novels. The big local favorite is *Dinner at Antoine's.* Keyes was much on the move, and the house holds several collections that she gathered on her travels. Among the most interesting is her gorgeous fan collection—aids to flirting and coquetry from all over the world—Chinese fans, Japanese fans, dramatic Spanish ones, and flowery French. Her collection of rare, very small French teapots of Limoges, Sevres, and English manufacture is one of only two such collections in the world. Keyes also amassed a fabulous collection of dolls. It and a manorial Victorian doll's house have become a special attraction for guests and their children.

The Beauregard-Keyes House is the place to come at Christmas time. Every year, the museum hosts the Doll's Tea Party on the second Saturday of December. Children of all ages are invited to bring their dolls to have tea with the dolls of the collection. Your doll is invited with your child, too.

PLANTATIONS AND THE FOOD EMPIRE

The mid-18th to 19th centuries saw New Orleans settled by a variety of immigrants: The Spanish, the English, Germans, Acadians, and Italians added ethnic diversity to the basic Louisiana French formula, and with the settlers' industry and the fertile land around them, not to mention a port, the foundation for the plantation era was laid.

These settlers, discovering rich lands bordering the Mississippi River, quickly began moving out of the city of New Orleans to seek fortunes in planting. At the time it was said that it took only three good crops to make a millionaire. Little stood in the way of this goal, as nearly everywhere along the river were fertile grounds for three cash crops that would prosper with the merest husbandry. These were sugarcane, cotton, and rice.

Large land grants available to the early settler came with only one stipulation—that the settler build a home and plant a crop within one year. Many an aspiring planter came with a fortune and a higher education as backing, as well as a hunger for wealth. Within a single generation, the people from these many backgrounds began to intermarry. With the passage of time, and crops having been successful, these Creole families grew in size and importance, and by the antebellum period many had built mansions almost as magnificent as they thought themselves, and reflecting the success of their (and their slaves') way with the land.

The layout of the typical plantation home was reduced to a simple formula. It had to be on or near the river and equipped with imposing white columns (that would photograph well in motion pictures to come). Normally, oak or magnolia trees were planted in an alley formation leading up to the door, and the house itself was flanked by outbuildings such as kitchens (often in separate buildings owing to fear of fire and the oppressive heat), dovecotes, or slave quarters. Behind the house were thousands of acres of sugarcane or cotton or perhaps indigo, with sugar mills or cotton gins to process these important crops. Some plantations reached an imposing degree of self-sufficiency. By 1855 there were more millionaires to be found between Natchez, Mississippi, and New Orleans than in the rest of the country put together. In New Orleans usage of the day, Creole could sometimes mean extravagant; it always meant fancy.

One plantation owner, with an annual income of well over $100,000, served 10-course dinners, everything from fish to coffee and wine to cigars, raised on his own plantation. He also transported his guests from New Orleans on a private steamboat. As a group, the landed aristocracy luxuriated in a lifestyle nearly unknown since the heyday of Rome.

The preparations for a Creole plantation wedding ranged from dreamlike straight into the realm of the unbelievable. The fortnight before the double wedding of two of his daughters, one doting father had many huge spiders imported from China. He had them set loose along the allée of trees leading to his house a few days before the wedding, so that they spun a wispy filament of webs across the dome of the natural arcade of trees. The father then had teams of young slaves dressed as cupids and armed with bellows blow gold dust onto the filament. When the 2,000 wedding guests arrived, their ornate carriages rolled over Persian rugs spread beneath the canopy of sparkling golden webs.

Most of the plantation houses of the 19th century provided for the needs of as many as 500 hands, free and slave.

Plantation owners traveled extensively, saw much, and came home with ideas; the plantation was fertile ground for botanical experimentation. Slaves at Oak Alley Plantation in Vacherie, for instance, were encouraged to experiment with horticulture whenever possible. A working slave, known to us only as Antoine, developed the world-famous paper-shell pecan here.

Back in New Orleans, there is something of a hint of this plantation food and style; and the very venue provides a provocative setting of contrasts.

CAFÉ ATCHAFALAYA

901 Louisiana Ave. (Garden District)
Tel. 504/891–5271

The Formica decor is plain, but the stuffed pork chops with corn-bread dressing, fried green tomatoes, and black-eyed peas will have you thinking you are eating a plantation menu—though not the sort Scarlett O'Hara cut her teeth on. If you come in a group, someone must try the soulful chicken and dumplings, as well as the fresh fruit cobblers that are out of this world. This is the taste of the Old South.

If you are interested in finding plantations and table arrangements more akin to Scarlett O'Hara's settings, the way to go is clearly mapped out for you on the Great River Road. A proper passage of plantations and the foods of this civilization can be made if you have even two days to put together. But three are better. Maybe four?

The Great River Road is not as scenic as you might think; in many places, industrial plants mar the landscape on one side of the road, and the levee obstructs the view of the Mississippi on the other. The road is known variously as U.S. 61 and Louisiana Routes 44 and 75 on the east bank of the river, and Louisiana Route 18 on the west bank. From the center of New Orleans, you can bypass some of the less appealing stretches by taking I–10 to I–310, which takes you to the River Road near Destrehan.

DESTREHAN PLANTATION

13034 River Rd.
Destrehan, LA 70047
Tel. 504/764–9315

Built in 1787, Destrehan is the oldest plantation house in the lower Mississippi Valley still intact. It is only a half hour from New Orleans off I–310 west (there are signs as you get close). A commodious West Indies–style mansion with white columns across the front, it projects a good idea of what sort of civilization grew up on the banks of the Mississippi. As you pull in off the road toward the house, the river's levee is just to your right. Destrehan is typical of the plantations built by the gentry, grown rich from cotton and indigo, as monuments to themselves. Alas, there is no restaurant.

SAN FRANCISCO

LA Rte. 44
Garyville, LA 70051
Tel. 504/535–2341

Twenty minutes up Route 44, the elaborate steamboat Gothic house, built in 1853, has a Creole-style exposed upper gallery. There's an unusual louvered roof, ornate millwork, and colorful painted ceilings. It was originally called St. Frusquin, from the French slang term, *sans fruscins,* meaning "without a penny in my pocket," the condition in which the owner found himself after paying the construction costs. If your time is limited, press on, as there is no restaurant; that very interesting upper gallery feature does make it worth a gander from the road, at least.

From San Francisco, turn left, downriver, on Route 44. Follow it to Route 53, turn left, and turn left again when you reach U.S. 61 and follow it until you turn left for the new Lutcher-Wallace Bridge. On the other side of the bridge, follow Route 18 about 3 miles upriver to Vacherie. If you'd rather take a ferry and drive the other side of the river after you leave San Francisco, turn left on 44, turn right onto the ferry landing at the intersection of Route 53, ride the ferry (runs every half hour) across to Route 18, where you turn right, and drive about 15 miles to Vacherie.

LAURA PLANTATION

2247 Hwy. 18
Vacherie, LA 70090
Tel. 504/265–7690

At Vacherie are the ramshackle remains of Laura Plantation, named for the 1805 owner-manager, Laura Procul. One of the plantation's claims to fame is Uncle Remus; the Br'er Rabbit stories on which Joel Chandler Harris based his book are said to have been first told in the United States here by Senegalese slaves. It's not an opulent showplace, to be sure—but the six slave cabins are still up, and partially restored. The whole site is under reconstruction and will eventually show us in what conditions slaves lived in this part of the Old South. It's interesting to poke around even now, though it smells of dilapidation and oppression, and there is no restaurant.

OAK ALLEY PLANTATION

Vacherie, LA 70090
Tel. 504/265–2151

Farther west on Route 18, you enter the mainstream of the old aristocratic South at the gate of the Oak Alley Plantation. The place where Antoine created the paper-shell pecan,

Oak Alley is more famous today for its eponymous stand of trees. Built in 1837, the house is approached down its magnificent alley of 28 matched live oaks that date from the early 1700s and easily outdo the mere 12 oaks of *Gone with the Wind.* They are spectacular to see; to drive under them in a convertible, even with the top down, is to drive in the shade. A National Historic Landmark, Oak Alley has the most spectacular setting in the entire Mississippi Valley, which is quite a fair piece. The plantation is open for tours daily; you must stand on the balcony looking out on the trees. A café (breakfast and lunch only), gift shop, and overnight cabins now cater to visitors.

There are so many plantations of note on the Great River Road that it's like visiting the châteaux of the Loire. The Lutcher-Wallace bridge at Vacherie will take you across the river to U.S. 61, from which you return to Route 44 and turn west, upriver, toward Tezcuco Plantation and Houmas House.

TEZCUCO PLANTATION

3138 Hwy. 44
Darrow, LA 70725
Tel. 504/562–3929

Tezcuco is a raised Greek Revival cottage. Its main floor sits above a high masonry basement story, a style borrowed from earlier French Colonial houses. Dating from 1855 (from the building boom, you can see what kind of wealth was around here then), named with an Aztec Indian word meaning resting place, and trimmed with wrought-iron galleries, it, too, is on the National Register of Historic Places. Charming hostesses lead daily tours; there is a gift shop that sells homemade dolls created by the owner, an antiques shop, and overnight cabins. The restaurant, open for breakfast and lunch, offers such enticing plantation fare as crawfish étouffée. The version here is spicy and Cajun (with rounds of spicy sausage as well as the crustacean) and served on a bed of fluffy white rice. Equally a Cajun treat is the chicken and sausage jambalaya: the classic, with plenty of personality because of the cayenne (instead of black) pepper. Shrimp Creole is for the inveterate explorer: The shrimp is served in a clinging red piquant sauce that will adhere to your taste buds with a searing vengeance. The Cajun seafood pasta consists of whatever the day's catch brings in served in an enticing béchamel sauce. Here are some other favorites of the house: pork roast, seasoned, glazed, and baked with onions and mashed potatoes;

and smothered pork chops under vegetables and steamed onions, with mashed potatoes drizzled with gravy.

HOUMAS HOUSE AND GARDENS

40136 Hwy., 942 Burnside
Darrow, LA 70725
Tel. 504/522–2262

This is a splendid Greek Revival mansion, so à la mode in 1840, the year it was built. It was completely restored in 1940 and now has guides in antebellum dress. The rooms are square, of generous proportions, and furnished with period antiques. As you walk in, you feel as if you were entering the

19th century. There is no restaurant now, but Houmas House was a favorite destination for visitors in the mid-19th century, when it served as a sort of genteel hotel, where the "right sort of people" took a break in a longer journey and enjoyed syllabub, a drink made from milk, curdled by wine or cider and sweetened. There is an elegant formal garden where you can stroll or sit and rest after your tour.

Now you know what it's like to live on a first-class plantation. Continue upriver on Route 44 until you come to the Sunshine Bridge. Cross it and follow along Louisiana Route 1 upriver past Donaldsonville to where more plantations await.

NOTTOWAY PLANTATION

30970 Hwy. 405
White Castle, LA 70788
Tel. 504/525–2730

Two miles north of White Castle is Nottoway—a National Historic Landmark and the largest plantation home in the South. Since its completion in 1859 it has been known as the White Castle of the South. Indeed, it dwarfs the White House. If it is true that the Louisiana plantations on the Mississippi are America's châteaux of the Loire, Nottoway is Chenonceaux. It is a skyscraper among plantations; the white, columned mansion rises higher than the surrounding oaks and has 200 windows, 165 doors, and 64 rooms (13 of which are let for overnight accommodations). There are guided tours, a gift shop, and a restaurant. Among the many good dishes served here, the oyster-artichoke soup is especially delicious:

NOTTOWAY'S OYSTER-ARTICHOKE SOUP

½ lb. butter

½ cup chopped onion

½ cup chopped celery

1 pt. chicken stock

1 cup quartered cooked artichoke hearts

1 qt. fresh oysters, chopped

1 qt. heavy cream

1 pt. half-and-half

In a large saucepan melt the butter, onion, and celery and simmer for 5 minutes. Add the chicken stock and cook on low heat for 15 minutes. Add the artichokes and oysters, and simmer for 10 minutes longer. Finally, add the cream and half-and-half. Heat thoroughly for 15 minutes on low heat. (Do not boil.) Serves 12.

Choose your wine wisely—maybe a spicy Muscadet.

It would be wise to stay over at Nottoway and start out fresh in the morning with a keen appetite because we've saved the best for last. Retrace your way back down Route 1 to Donaldsonville, but don't recross the bridge this time; halt just at its approach and follow the shoreline a few hundred yards upriver to Lafitte's Landing.

LAFITTE'S LANDING RESTAURANT

11275 Hwy. 70, Sunshine Bridge Access Rd.
Donaldsonville, LA 70346
Tel. 504/473–1232

Here the celebrated John Folse holds forth; you may have seen his "Taste of Louisiana" cooking series on public television. He is one of America's most acclaimed chefs, having received the honor of National Chef of the Year from the American Culinary Foundation and having had his Lafitte's Landing Restaurant inducted into the Fine Dining Hall of Fame (one of only 10 American restaurants so honored). In 1989, Folse was invited to create a Vatican state dinner in Rome. At this Cajun, Creole, New Orleans–style dinner, the Pope confided to Folse, upon meeting the chef, that his favorite food in America was gumbo. Folse's splendid establishment, a raised Acadian cottage in the shadow of the Sunshine Bridge, a former residence of the buccaneer Jean Lafitte, is faultlessly and imaginatively restored. It offers Cajun, Creole, and French cuisine. There is a wonderful collection of art on the walls, and it is one of the few places where you can get dinner in the area (but call first). Here's the recipe for Folse's thick, flavorful gumbo.

LOUISIANA SEAFOOD GUMBO

½ lb. 35-count shrimp, peeled and deveined

½ lb. jumbo lump crabmeat

1 dozen shucked oysters, liquid reserved

½ cup vegetable oil

¾ cup flour

1 cup chopped onions

½ cup chopped celery

½ cup chopped bell pepper

⅛ cup diced garlic

½ lb. sliced andouille sausage

½ lb. claw crabmeat

1½ qts. shellfish stock, hot

1 cup sliced green onions

⅛ cup chopped parsley

Salt and cayenne pepper to taste

Louisiana Gold sauce to taste

In a 1-gallon stock pot, heat oil over medium-high heat. The oil hot, add flour and stir with a wire whisk until a brown roux is achieved. Do not allow the roux to burn. Should black specks appear, discard the roux and start over. Once the roux is golden, add onions, celery, bell pepper, and garlic. Sauté about 3 to 5 minutes, or until the vegetables are wilted. Add sausage, blend well into vegetable mixture, and sauté an additional 2 to 3 minutes. Stir the claw crabmeat into the mixture; this will begin the seafood flavor process. Slowly add hot shellfish stock, one ladleful at a time, stirring constantly until all is incorporated. Bring to a low boil, reduce to a simmer, and let cook about 30 minutes. Add additional stock, if necessary, to maintain volume. Add green onions and parsley and season to taste with salt, pepper, and Louisiana Gold. Fold shrimp, lump crabmeat, oysters, and reserved liquid into soup. Return to low boil and cook about 5 minutes more. Adjust seasonings and serve over cooked rice. Serves 6.

You want perfection?—ya gotta work! You'd rather have somebody else do it?—walk into the restaurant. Inside Lafitte's Landing, the inviting breath of fresh air-conditioning dries off the humidity. The elements and the decor conspire to welcome you. Cool brick walls are covered with paintings—New Orleans scenes, contemporary European works—and polished floors are padded with Oriental carpeting. Immediately, a mint julep is suggested by the maître d'. Take it; you have never had one like this before. I see the leaves being hand-ground at the bar. With hints of Chartreuse, it is like a puree of pine forest and is delicious.

Thus refreshed, we are left to deliberate the menu. Then come, unrequested, assorted *amuse gueules* (hors d'oeuvres), here, an elegant tent of shrimp in sweet and pungent garlic butter. Next comes an eggplant crepe stuffed with oyster mushrooms (these have plenty of taste), buttery and topped with a blue edible flower (dianthus). These engaging proposals make us take our menus seriously, formulate our choices.

We will take the crawfish boil. I have heard so much of this that it is time to try it from the hand of a master chef. And it's time to test a food maxim: A good meal, like a good restaurant, must have a good soup. The boil comes, like a soup, in an elegant bowl. Containing corn, crawfish, and bell pepper and potato pieces, it is spicy and flavorful, a little like a good New England chowder. Boil, in fact, is the clambake of Louisiana, and a social common denominator, a way for people to meet and mix.

This broth, however, is more flavorful—enticing. Yes, it's made with crawfish, but the preparation uses bell peppers in a particular way. In the right amount, they give a sweetness to the soup that is almost translucent; that leads you on to taste and taste again. It is an effect of the *relevé* technique in cooking. When strong-flavored ingredients, such as peppers, garlic, and certain herbs, are cooked, the heat can often drive all or some of the oil out of them. To counteract this, near the end of the cooking, they are relevéed: A like quantity of the same ingredient is added to bolster the final flavor. The final flavor effect, then, comes from two tastes overlaid—one very fresh, the other a little faded. Multiply by the number of spices in the dish, and you'll get some idea of its taste complexity.

Next comes an étouffée of crab, buttery and spicy, and vegetable lasagna. I decided to try the latter because my maternal grandmother, who was Italian, lived with us for a while and would have curled her lip at the idea. It is chewy but tender. The palm for lasagna, however, still rests with my grandma. A word about the service: It is quiet, unobtrusive, but warm and friendly.

Finally, it comes: alligator *médaillons au beurre blanc* (round or oval slices in white butter sauce). The medallions—more like scallopini—are under a layer of crab (again, the Creole two-taste principle). They are chewy but savory. No, alligator does not taste like chicken; it's sweet and fishy, more like big game fish than anything else.

I must say that the meal at Lafitte's Landing was the high point of my New Orleans food exploration. It had balance, achievement; the chef takes risks. It is like anything else in any art: Unless failure is risked, results are often pedestrian.

Notwithstanding, everything about the meal at Lafitte's Landing was stable, as if the results could have been predicted by the chef, were achieved through his intervention, and were the total expression of his original intentions. Speaking of stability, the average length of service for the wait staff at Lafitte's Landing is 9 to 15 years.

THE CAJUNS

When most people who don't live in New Orleans think of its food, they think Cajun, but the Big Easy is the capital of Creole, not Cajun, with some notable exceptions. To wake up the taste—and maybe to sharpen the critical sense—we will begin this Cajun food cruise with a middle-rung restaurant assessment. I have heard it said, as it is said of Paris, that you can't get a bad meal in New Orleans. Well, to start, and to better judge what follows, we are going to put this fable to the test. We will hit a neighborhood restaurant: one unpatrolled by food-critic fat cats, one where real folks dine, in the heart of the Quarter, one where you'd be likely to stumble inside without any preamble, advance guidance, or direction, to see what gives. It's a place extremely popular with the locals; where they go when they have a few extra dollars and really don't need very much more.

TUJAGUE'S

823 Decatur St. (French Quarter)
Tel. 504/525–8676

If your Louisiana excursion is not taking you to Cajun country (100–150 miles west of New Orleans) Tujague's may be the place for you; the menu specializes in Creole and Cajun, offering a traditional six-course table d'hôte menu with four entrée choices nightly. So you can tour southern Louisiana, gastronomically speaking, without ever leaving your chair. Perhaps it is because this place is such a time-saver that it beckons so invitingly from its corner location to the tourist crowd with a big neon sign and a wide, well-worn bar that wraps around the room.

In the dining room, the white-and-gray hexagonal tile flooring is the sort that was once so popular in barber shops, and I seat myself in trepidation that I am about to get my locks shorn. There is a picture wall displaying hundreds of former clients and an undistinguished wine at the head of the wine list does little to stimulate the appetite or imagination. The bar Chardonnay is garbage, the service is unapologetic and unenthusiastic, and altogether I feel that the dining experience I am about to (enjoy?) is not apt to be singular. The room, however, does fill up—mostly large parties, families, doubtless come to graze on opportunities of price, rather than excellence, and the place begins to be convivial.

I have an inspiration. I order beer—Bass ale is on tap. I also order Creole soup and shrimp *rémoulade* (mayonnaise sauce with herbs); this is such a New Orleans staple I decide to sample it now, if only to make comparisons later. The shrimp rémoulade comes first on a bed of salad and is simple and gross, the lettuce crude-cut with no finesse, the sauce greasy, with the taste of mayo from the bottle, and the shrimp wet and clunky. After the rémoulade I am convinced that you *can* get a bad meal in New Orleans.

The Creole soup, however, seems to bring the restaurant back and justify, somewhat, the crowds at the doors. It is thick enough to coat a spoon and piquant and flavorful. I shake on some of the Tabasco sauce from the bottle on my table, and it is even better.

My palate tingling, I am eager to taste the jambalaya. The sausage in Tujague's preparation is hot (as in spicy, Spanish), and the customers seem to like it that way. Jambalaya is much happier with beer, which is not overwhelmed by the spiciness, than with wine. There is very little grumbling or silence in the room once meals have been served, but much laughing.

Tujague's may not be for those who come to New Orleans and only want to taste the best, but by all means, go to Tujague's, mingle with the crowd, drink beer, eat the jambalaya, and forget everything else.

If you do want to taste the best in Louisiana-style food, there is one restaurant that heads the list:

K-PAUL'S LOUISIANA KITCHEN

416 Chartres St. (French Quarter)
Tel. 504/524–7394

Through rapid-fire word-of-mouth and favorable national publicity (the chef became a media king), K-Paul's Louisiana Kitchen became, in the 1980s, New Orleans's hottest restaurant. There is so much pressure to get in, that would-be diners willingly stand in the street. This is the price of popularity and excellence. Everybody's dying to get in to taste the splendors of chef Paul Prudhomme's cuisine. At any rate, admission inside K-Paul's redbrick walls has become, for many, the essence of a food visit to New Orleans; some go as far as to say you haven't been to New Orleans unless you've eaten at K-Paul's.

Far from being oppressive under the weight of this sterling reputation, the atmosphere of K-Paul's is completely unprepossessing and uncomplicated—laid-back and relaxed. They ask you what you want; they make suggestions; you get it. With the down-home approach here, some dishes are the simplest yet most surprising creations you'll find in the city. Many have their roots in Cajun country.

At our visit to K-Paul's, we're seated in a big, pleasant, brick-lined room. We start with the green gumbo. The color comes from collard greens, mustard greens, spinach, and sometimes cabbage. The gumbo is *very* green, comes in a thick cup, has a tomato base, and with its crab, rice, and garlic could easily

make itself a habit. We go on to drink the local beer, Abita, a snappy amber ale that's a welcome change from the national blands. It goes well with a course of scallops and pasta; the piquant sauce served with it breaks through the blotter food I ordered to set me up for one of the city's most famous dishes, one that helped chef Prudhomme make his reputation. I didn't want to tackle the world-famous dish too hungry. Redfish is almost all fished out these days, so what chef Paul offers as an alternative to blackened redfish is blackened tuna. It comes with mashed potatoes; save room for it because the serving is immense. The potatoes are full of nutty warmth, the tuna is thick and chewy,

almost with a red meat flavor. That's Prudhomme's food—natural food, prepared to bring out its natural goodness. No, there's no room for dessert—not even sweet potato pecan pie with Chantilly cream—and it is with regrets, but with full stomachs and memories of luscious green gumbo, that we depart.

For real Cajun food you have to go to Cajun country. And where might Cajun country be? you ask. Do you have a few hours, or days, to spare?

Morning shines through a milky mid-May sky, washed by a rain. We leave the city driving westward on I–10, along Esplanade Ridge, a row of fine houses near the I–10 airport exit. When we stop for coffee on the way, I learn something more revealing about New Orleans customs and attitudes: After saying good morning, the next words you can expect from a New Orleanian are, "Where'd ya eat?"

ATCHAFALAYA BASIN

From I–10, you turn south onto I–310, a smooth, concrete ribbon, around and through which is set and suspended a Spanish moss–hung jungle and cypress forest. It's all wild and natural, and just the thing that you came here to find. The ground is flat and rich in black soil and sugarcane; rice,

pecans, and seafood round out the larder. We head toward one of the great, natural, wild regions of America. The sky is now broad and very bright; the waters are filled with great crested herons, their necks stretching out like snakes in the sun. In less than an hour we cross the Mississippi and are in the Atchafalaya River basin. This pristine area is rich in wildlife—the place where most of Louisiana's crawfish historically come from. All around you are crawfish farms and their signs.

Among the things people don't catch in the Atchafalaya, and there are excluder devices in the traps to prevent them from doing so, are turtles. There are turtle farms here, but the take is controlled and mainly for restaurants. The Atchafalaya is the best place on earth to discover the savoriness of turtle soup.

From I–310 we head west on U.S. Route 90 toward St. Martinville and Lafayette, in search of other taste experiences. First we come to Avery Island—not really an island but a salt plug (a place where the salt came up through the earth and made a salt dome). Avery is worth a visit for a special food reason, as it is home to the very special condiment we seek: Tabasco, a kind of pepper sauce. Put up exclusively by **McIlhenny and Company** (Avery Island, LA 70513, tel. 318/365–8173), it has been drawing tears and pleasing palates for 120 years. People come a long way to see where the hot is made. In the predawn, school buses start lining up to deposit their little charges in a waiting room filled with brochures and propaganda. There is a lecture followed by a film. The subject is pepper; Avery Island pepper—Tabasco. It is this the kids have been driven three hours to see and hear. But this is Louisiana where the favorite subject is food, and they all like it hot.

The factory's short film tells you the story of Tabasco: McIlhenny was a New Orleans banker who, like many of his 19th-century contemporaries, dabbled in some of the natural sciences; his was botany. Having received some interesting pepper seeds from Mexico, he developed a variety of pepper himself—very small, very hot, and bright red—which became the base for Tabasco sauce. Tabasco sauce combines naturally occurring Avery Island ground salt in solution with crushed and mashed Avery Island pepper, and a fermentation process ensues. A *chapeau* (crust) develops on the surface of the pepper brew. The fluid is then drained off at the bottom of the vat, blended with vinegar, and sealed in bottles, which are sold in more than 100 countries as Tabasco sauce.

After the film, you can view the bottling—a long line of jiggling bottles streams down a conveyer belt—and buy the product. A mini sample is handed out free. It's not large enough to season a hamburger, however; most Louisianans hang it from their rear-view mirror.

Wanna take a bite out of crime? Not so fast. A different solution comes from Avery Island: Red pepper spray is offered at $9.95. "Why put up with crime?" local ads ask. Another hot tip: Mix paint with Tabasco—it keeps the barnacles off the bottom of your boat. Now you know what potent stuff this hot pepper sauce is. It's even said to aid digestion.

Onward then, back across U.S. Route 90 toward New Iberia. Crossing into southwestern Louisiana, which stretches from Lake Charles to Baton Rouge, you enter an area that can be only called "special." Gas stations sell crawfish; car washes, ditto. There's usually a line outside each establishment, and the crawfish seem to come in at $4 a pound. The duck gumbos are "real good," and the Cajuns seem to prefer them because of the richness of the dark meat. Egrets wade at the side of the road. There are lots of armadillos; Cajuns say they're safe only because nobody has figured out how to stick a fork in them. "Cajun 'il eat anything that doesn't eat him first," is the local saying.

In **New Iberia,** 14 miles south of St. Martinville, billed as the capital of sugarcane country, is one of the South's most famous homes: The antebellum **Shadows-on-the-Teche** (317 E. Main St., tel. 318/369–6446) is worth a look inside for its dazzling, quirky architectural appointments. Across the street is a reasonable bed-and-breakfast, **Le Rosier** (314 E. Main St., tel. 318/367–5306). The **Conrad Rice Mill** (307 Ann St., tel. 318/364–7242), the country's oldest still-functioning such mill, is on the National Register of Historic Places. It dates from 1912 and produces a sensational wild pecan rice that you must try. At the same address, the rice mill's **Konriko Company Store** (tel. 318/367–6163) sells Cajun food and crafts.

Sweet potato stands are all over New Iberia. Hot on a napkin and with a pat of butter, sweet potatoes are just fine for taking away a little hunger. Popcorn rice is also plentiful, chewy and granular because it's unrefined; the bran is on, and so it's good for you. Rice cultivation is a natural on the prairie here because the land has a lot of clay in it, which holds water. Sugarcane in the fields awaits fall harvest and the annual festival. You can see sugar mills, which smell like burning caramel in the pan.

Now we are in the heart of Evangeline country, land to which Evangeline came and found heartbreak. Her journey to southern Louisiana, as for most Cajuns in those times, was arduous and took many years. About 1755, the French-speaking Acadians, then living in what is now Nova Scotia,

were driven from their homes by the British for refusing to renounce their religion (Catholic) and swear allegiance to the British crown. The men were separated from the women, put on 27 ships, and dispersed to the winds. This is part of the Cajun saga and the subject of the celebrated Longfellow poem, *Evangeline,* about the wanderings of Gabriel Lajeunesse, looking for Evangeline Bellefontaine, and of Evangeline, looking for Gabriel.

As Acadians were known as hard workers and good farmers, in time, their reputations caught up with them. The king of Spain invited them to move into what is now southern Louisiana. Here they found the French-speaking, citified Creoles, whose presence dated from the first days of exploration, as well as the several native North American tribes who already inhabited the area. The Acadians fell in with the Indians and from them learned how to sculpt pirogues out of cypress trees, and felt at home, skimming the waters like bugs on the dew. Rural by preference, they settled along the bayous and marshes and across the prairies, trapping, fishing, and farming Spanish land grants, and became the Cajuns. Small towns appeared and prospered.

At length, and still in search of her Gabriel, Evangeline reached St. Martinville—in the Cajun version of the story. As soon as she stepped from the boat, Gabriel saw her. And his

heart sank. He was forced to tell her what had happened during their long separation: He had found and betrothed himself to another.

In **St. Martinville,** north of New Iberia off U.S. Route 90, the 200-year-old Evangeline oak, the legendary meeting place of Evangeline and Gabriel, is a local landmark. It stands at the corner of Evangeline Boulevard and Bayou Teche, its branches spreading out over an entire lawn. A little band lounges here all day waiting to speak French and promote true Cajun sights and points of interest.

The inn across the street is the **Old Castillo Hotel** (La Place d'Evangeline, 220 Evangeline Blvd., St. Martinville, LA 70582, tel. 318/394–4010). After the 1789 revolution, French royalists came to the Castillo, a brick building (now on the National Register of Historic Places) with a second-story veranda, and were received with Southern warmth, a gracious menu, and balls and dancing. Now you can feast here on crawfish, catfish stuffed with lump crab meat, or corn and crab bisque. Fried alligator offers a touch of the exotic. There are also five large guest rooms, some with antiques, all with baths.

Even along the highway, the flavors of true Cajun are signposted. Everything is tied up with food, stuff for the Cajun pot; everybody cooks or sells food around here. Sign in a gas station: BOUDIN $1.09/LINK OR HOT LINK $1.29. Yes, it's sure, we are in Cajun country now. You've got to come all the way here for the real thing.

For a quick swing through a big Cajun town, stop in **Lafayette,** known as the "Capital of Acadiana." It is the terminus of U.S. Route 90. With a population of about 100,000, it is larger than you might expect. You'll find Hilton, Gateway, Comfort, and Holiday inns here. For cultural diversion and fact-finding, it has art galleries such as the **Lafayette** (412 Travis St., tel. 318/269–0363), a focal point for local artists that exhibits and sells fine arts and crafts, including pottery and sculptures. The **Artists Alliance** gallery (125 W. Vermilion St., tel. 318/233–7518) has work by such local painters as Frances Pavy. The museums in town are a bit more ambitious: The **Lafayette Natural History Museum** (637 Girard Park Dr., tel. 318/268–5544) has exhibits ranging from insects to dinosaurs plus planetarium shows. The **Mississippi Valley Museum** (200 Greenleaf Dr., tel. 318/981–2364) displays artifacts of local Native Americans (pottery, dugout canoes) backed up by Robert Dafford paintings of Indian village life and demonstrations such as the making of fire by rubbing two sticks together and the art of using the blow gun. **Acadian Village** (200 Greenleaf Dr., tel. 318/981–2364), a folk life museum, has self-guided tours of 19th-century homes kept as they were originally.

If you're in Lafayette around lunch time, you might want to take a moment for:

DWYER'S CAFÉ
323 Jefferson St.
Lafayette, LA
Tel. 318/235–9364

They have burgers and Cajun platters, but take the hot buffet: pork roast with eggplant; rice and gravy (a real Southern treat); or Friday's crawfish étouffée or shrimp in rice, smothered in okra, gravy, and butter.

North of Lafayette, off I–49, is **Carencro,** where Enola Prudhomme's Cajun Café is located. Enola is the Queen of Cajun, famous sister of the famous Paul Prudhomme, and she has many interesting stories about Cajun cooking. Better, she sets a true Cajun table, and who wants to drive straight through lunchtime with a Cajun restaurant so handy?

ENOLA PRUDHOMME'S CAJUN CAFÉ
4676 N.E. Evangeline Thruway (I–49, 7 mi north of I–10)
Carencro, LA
Tel. 318/896–7964

Its white clapboard sides appear abruptly off the road, surrounded by an immense parking lot. Inside, the place is an enormous, pine-paneled, air-conditioned, L-shape room. Enola is an intense, dark-haired woman. Ever the hostess, she comes over to sit with us, to guide us through our choices, to better explain her cuisine—how it came about—as her foods are served.

"Always did the cookin'," she says of her farm background. "I was one of thirteen children, but I hated house-

work." Enola made a deal with her mother. If she got let off from chores, 'Nola would be responsible for all the meals for the family. "All of 'em," she emphasizes, and there was no electricity in the house.

The food arrives, and we eat. A shrimp dish comes first, a sort of empanada, a doughy crust wrapping all inside with its juices and seasonings. It is good and tasty. Then we have the dish for which she is known: corn maquechoux. It is spicy and sweet—a caramelized yam crunch with bell peppers and corn, and worth the trip to the Café. We conclude: There is a lot of taste in this simple food served in such a straightforward manner. Further, it is low calorie—Enola has also written a low-calorie cookbook on Cajun techniques, available at her establishment and in other places.

Vermilionville, just north of Lafayette on I–49 (watch out, Louisiana troopers are alert), is a replica of 18th-century Lafayette. Its buildings re-create a Cajun village of 1755; they're furnished with authentic period pieces and inhabited by folk living the life the Cajuns lived. They will show you something of this life and what the Cajuns did for entertainment. There is music, singing, dancing, and Cajun cooking.

Inside the admissions gate, Vermilionville stretches out in nearly 20 buildings. We ask directions and repair immediately to the on-site **Prejean's Cajun Cooking School** (3480 Hwy. 167N, Lafayette, LA 70508, tel. 318/896–3247), where a woman dressed in folk costume is conducting a cooking class. A few burners and a big black pot are nearby. She sets a skillet on one of the burners, lights it, and pours in some oil. When it is bubbling, she puts in some shrimp, all the time commenting on what she is doing and responding to questions from the audience that is seated around her on wooden folding chairs. After a moment's cooking, and pulling the shrimp heads from their tails, she sets the shrimp on a plate, salts and peppers them, and passes the plate around. They are sweet and delicious.

Although she doesn't use it in her demonstration, next she explains the pot, and another Louisiana staple, okra. "It [the pot] is for the roux," she says, "brought here by the Cajuns." After explaining that roux is the base of all Cajun cooking, she talks about okra. Okra is an African vegetable, she tells us; it was brought here by the blacks. So the Cajuns put it in the pot. The black pot itself comes from Haiti.

Across the way from the Cajun Cooking School is a dance hall; a crowd of people is dancing to lively rhythms, and we are invited to join them. If there's one concept that describes the Cajuns, it should be just that—join together.

Next, you can drive to **Breaux Bridge,** just 10 miles east on I–10 from Lafayette (take exit 109). Breaux Bridge bills itself as the "Crawfish Capital of the World!" If you visit during the first full weekend in May, you'll see why—every year, the inhabitants of Breaux Bridge set out to prove their claim with a crawfish festival. They also set a mean crawfish table, or tables, overflowing with the miniature lobsters and crawfish items. There are étouffées, gumbos, and crawfish pies—in ways you never dreamed of cooking the crustacean—and much of it is free. There are Cajun cooking, singing, and dancing, and some very friendly people. For more information, call the Breaux Bridge Chamber of Commerce (tel. 318/332–6655).

For a place to stay in town you can try:

BAYOU BED AND BREAKFAST CABINS
Breaux Bridge, LA 70517
Tel. 318/332–6158

It ain't fancy—you'll think you're staying in a movie with Walter Brennan—but the restaurant features genuine "Boudin and Cracklin," and it's right on the bayou.

From Breaux Bridge, you can follow I–10 eastward 44 miles to **Baton Rouge.** Here you can see the 1932 *moderne* state capitol building, the tallest in the Union, and a fine naval military museum aboard the destroyer USS *Kidd* docked along the Mississippi riverbank. Across from the destroyer, the old state capitol building, a Gothic Revival structure from 1849, boasts the finest rococo-style staircase in North America, and other architectural flourishes.

Baton Rouge is a good base for continued Cajun excursions, as Cajunland is all around it: Up north a bit (Rte. 61, 16 miles) is St. Francisville, listed in the National Register of Historic Places. Chartered during Spanish rule, it's the prettiest town in the state—a place to stroll the streets and discover the sights serendipitously.

One of the most rewarding things you can do in southern Louisiana is to visit a bayou restaurant. "Bayou" is an Indian word that means creek with a very slow flow. The most appetizing bayou I know to visit is the Maringouin. It runs through the town of **Livonia** 35 miles northwest of Baton Rouge on U.S. Route 190. You will find your images of the South reflected in its still waters, in the white clapboard buildings on its banks, in the shawls of gray Spanish moss hanging from twisted old oaks and, of course, in the good food.

JOE'S "DREYFUS STORE" RESTAURANT

2731 Maringouin Rd. W
Livonia, LA
Tel. 504/637–2625

As you make the left turn onto Route 411 off U.S. Route 190, the bayou stretches out before you, smooth as glass. The restaurant is just set back from the road, on the right, its white facade reflected in the waters. Park in the lot to its right and scale the wooden steps. The place was once a dry-goods store, and there are still old apothecary tables and artifacts lying helter-skelter that give it an undeniable charm. If you arrive at 9 PM, it will be crowded; 8:30 is best, before the kitchen slows down and the choices narrow. The owners, Dianne and Joe Major, and their staff are the most polite people in the world. As you would expect in the Atchafalaya Basin, both catfish and crawfish are on the menu at Joe's, but here you can have them on the same plate: The humongous fish comes to the table with its tail perpendicular to the plate and fried to a crisp; the head is buried in a stack of crab and crawfish atop a bed of rice, looking like Moby Dick diving into a mountain of crustaceans.

Even with the healthiest of appetites you will not finish this, so generous is the portion. They will offer a bottle of Tabasco sauce to sprinkle on. Use it; it aids in digestion. The price of this miraculous feast? $14.95. What to drink? I stick with Abita beer and find it still saucy and fragrant.

There are other sumptuous, reasonably priced Louisiana treats to enjoy at Joe's: Fresh, steamed artichoke, in butter sauce—hot or cold—is a measly $3.50, the crawfish bisque $3.95. And there is the crawfish special, their tails rémoulade, étouffée (over steamed rice), and fried. With this you have the right to the delicious bisque—a complete dinner—all for $14.95. There is jumbo (believe it) Gulf shrimp, boiled in garlic butter, with lemon and parsley, and served with potatoes and vegetables—as is everything at Joe's—for $13.95. If you're tired of seafood, they have prime rib of beef, slow roasted to perfection, with cream horseradish sauce: regular cut, $11.95; king size, $14.95. But if you would be a true food explorer you have to try the fresh Louisiana frogs' legs—deep-fried or sautéed Provençale (garlic and tomatoes) style—for $12.95. Either way, they are buttery and succulent. There are "fresh and fat" soft-shell crabs—deep-fried or sautéed (even Marylanders have to try them this way) and jumbo sized—for $8. But who can, or should, escape Louisiana without tasting the pork? Marinated, very tender and extra lean, charbroiled pork tenderloin on a bed of braised red cabbage will be served to you at $10.95. If you

like game, there's fresh quail in season—which means fall. Served in Port wine sauce, it comes to the table at $7.50, but is only $11.95 for a pair if there are two of you.

All in all it's a perfect night; the food is wonderful, the staff congenial. And the waitress's name is Scarlett. Really.

In this Cajun expedition we have seen everything these people are truly known for—fresh produce, simply cooked, in unusual combinations. A true rural people, they eat what they find around them. Against this, although they offer some excellent individual dishes, the so-called Cajun restaurants of New Orleans seem but a pale shadow.

CAJUN FRENCH AND CREOLE FRENCH

The two main thrusts of the New Orleans food empire —its most enduring and stable—are Cajun French and Creole French. Cajuns and Creoles alike speak the French language, but that is about all they have in common. The cuisine that the Cajuns produced did not grow out of their French heritage, but from this new experience and place. It was natural, economical, and simple; the basis was an improvisational creativity with the natural raw materials at hand.

The Creole French, on the other hand—those arriving after the French Revolution—came directly from France. They brought haute cuisine with them. True, they found superb ingredients new to them in their New Orleans home, but these they bent toward French treatment and taxonomy. What they produced was a complex cuisine that was sophisticated and artful and as elegant as themselves (just ask them). When ice became too expensive in the sultry, Southern capital (once going from $6 to $65 a pound), Creoles went as far as to sew broken glass into cheesecloth to float in water so it would tinkle in the glass. (Few guests noticed the trick.) In cuisine today they are also tricky. They put puff pastry around a costly black truffle; few notice the truffle is really an olive. But they are very charming, and their cuisine is full of surprises, and never too far from its French heritage.

Antoine's

713 St. Louis St. (French Quarter)
Tel. 504/581–4422

Founded in 1840, Antoine's is the oldest restaurant in the Big Easy. It is a stronghold of food classicism and Creole chauvinism down to its artichoke bottoms (which you must have with the eggs Sardou). Dining rooms are baroque; some glitter with dazzling crystal light. The extensive menu is written in French and could serve as a footnote for *Larousse Gastronomique.* It is a place to visit if you stick to certain old stan-

dards, the classics Antoine's is known for and could rarely ever ruin, no matter what the rush. Don't ask for variations on the main themes. The restaurant invented oysters Rockefeller in 1899, when John D. Rockefeller was the richest man in the world. And this is a suitably rich dish. The oysters are baked on the half shell in a cream sauce of pungent, pureed greens (not spinach) and dashed with anise liqueur. The exact proportions are a house secret, but the overall effect is marvelous. You should have your oysters Rockefeller here, for they are the best in the city. Most people have *pommes de terre soufflés* (potato puffs) served with this dish and follow their oysters with a crème caramel, and you should, too. It makes for one of the finest lunches or light dinners à l'Antoine's; be you a lavish tipper or not, you will be living like a Creole, and in New Orleans that's as good as it can get.

There are other staple entrées to choose for lunch or dinner at Antoine's. Crawfish bisque: Though it's a Cajun dish, one of the best in town is served at Antoine's (made with tomatoes, vegetables, stock, butter roux, and crawfish). Crawfish cardinal, crawfish tails served in ramekins with a zippy and tingling hot cream sauce, are fun. Beef tournedos: A boneless cut from the fillet section of the tenderloin (sometimes mistakenly called filet mignon, but there is only one mignon per tenderloin), these are usually the McCoys (plain fillets). You have your choice of three sauces: *marchand de vin* (red wine and garlic sauce usually stimulated with hot mustard and pepper); Bordelaise (red wine and shallots, but with poached beef marrow added); hollandaise (a bit buttery with beef; try one of the others). After eating pompano here, Cecil B. DeMille thundered, "Only God could have cooked that fish!"

For a special dessert, avoid something complicated like crêpes suzette and ask for Antoine's appropriately Creole crème brûlée. Not even indifference can ruin it. It's entertaining to watch the pure food theater practiced here, however. House lights dim repeatedly for the glow of the blue brandy flames of crêpes suzette and *café brûlot* (a filtered hot drink made from rum heated with sugar, cinnamon, an orange stuck with cloves, and lemon zest, into which scalding coffee has been poured). Antoine's can be the height of the elegant Creole dining experience; the brûlot is said to have brought tears to the eyes of the actress Helen Hayes.

The perspective of Antoine's will give us the vision to check out the French Creole:

GALATOIRE'S

209 Bourbon St. (French Quarter)
Tel. 504/525–2021

The setting, a narrow dining room with slow-turning, brass, multibulb ceiling fans, busy wallpaper, and green cur-

tains, is suggestive of an old-style Creole bistro, and that is exactly what Galatoire's is. Few customers, however, tire of squinting at the squiggly characters of the traditional menu. Trout amandine and crabmeat Yvonne are two of the finest seafood dishes to be had in the town, doubtless due to the care of the staff and quality of the produce. Creole bouillabaisse is saffronized and spicier than the French variety; veal or spring lamb chops in béarnaise sauce, which make for nearly perfect bistro food, come to the table quickly and in good order.

Don't let the easy decor of the place fool you; prices here come as a *coup de canon* (shock) for even New Orleans natives. Be sure to read the menu very closely and ask the waiter about specials. No matter how thick the Gallic atmosphere here, remember, the prices are not in francs.

Much of the recent craze in food these days—and New Orleans is a food place—has been generated by the Cajuns. The Creoles, however, were not about to just sit back and let their cousins from the sticks get all the attention. There are new and different things stirring in Creole cooking these days, as is proved by some of its leading New Orleans practitioners.

Emeril's

800 Tchoupitoulas St. (Warehouse District)
Tel. 504/528–9393

At Emeril's a fine Creole pedigree is at work; owner-chef Emeril Lagasse was formerly executive chef at the Commander's Palace. In 1990 Lagasse opened this cavernous and decidedly modern establishment that gives emphasis to Creole background and taste without disowning the rest of America. On the plate this comes across as a fresh corn crepe garnished with Louisiana caviar, or a sauté of crawfish on jambalaya cakes. You can grab a stool at the food bar and watch the chef and his staff put together your order. Don't leave without trying the fresh fruit cobbler, and, on your way out, get Emeril's cookbook, which is steeped in food history.

Not to concede anything, mind you, between Creole and Cajun, there is an interesting spot where the two rivals of the palate are combined in a war for your plate.

BRIGTSEN'S

723 Dante St. (Uptown)
Tel. 504/861–7610

Chef Frank Brigtsen, a protégé of Paul Prudhomme, holds forth here, producing food that fuses Creole elegance and Cajun earthiness. There is no question that Brigtsen succeeds in his proposition, and his ever-changing menu is followed by a virtual army of regulars who check it out every week or so. Reservations for the hard-pressed tables are therefore a must, sometimes as much as a week in advance. Everything that Frank proposes is fresh and smelling of the deep, complex tastes that smack of Creole-Cajun collaboration: You want cream of oyster soup? Very well, cream of oysters Rockefeller soup it is. Why not make it as a soup? It works. For the pure in heart, rabbit and chicken entrées are sauceless and bursting with their natural flavors. Lovers of Prudhomme's blackened tuna find it here in a trencherman's version—blackened prime rib; it comes under a spicy, toothsome charred coating. Fish dishes are likewise two-flavored, the second taste showing up under crawfish, shrimp, or oysters in buttery, spicy sauces. Roux-based gumbos are thick and dark here; one sees the hand of Prudhomme, and it is a powerful argument for the Cajun way with roux—the thicker and darker, the sweeter.

There is another very great cuisine (perhaps the greatest) present in New Orleans, which, in our haste to be all-inclusive, and may we roux the day, we have failed to mention so far on its own. It is at the bottom of all New Orleans pots, be they Cajun or Creole. Despite their differences, Creoles and Cajuns were French, from way back as far as it goes. For the Cajun, this was to the 16th century, when the first French fur trappers, fishermen, and explorers settled on the Gulf of St. Lawrence and along the St. Lawrence River. French cuisine is enjoying a renaissance in New Orleans today in some of the more imposing food temples, where the *cuisine du palais*—classic French cooking—is being offered (without, for the most part, Creole or Cajun influences) in all of its purity.

LOUIS XVI

St. Louis Hotel
730 Bienville St. (French Quarter)
Tel. 504/581–7000

Elegant sauces punctuate the bill of fare at this formal restaurant where men need to wear a jacket: Madeira sauce, red Bordelaise over beef, rosemary forced oil on vegetables. The wild, scintillating desserts are the ruminations of a baroque pastry chef. In all, it's the kind of meal you can have only in France, or New Orleans.

AFRICAN AND OTHER INFLUENCES

Besides French and Spanish settlers, New Orleans has benefited from the cooking lore of African, German, Irish, Italian, and Asian immigrants. Louisiana food, and New Orleans cuisine, is a melting pot of diverse cultures. New Orleans's location as a port on the Gulf of Mexico and terminus at the mouth of the Mississippi River allowed proponents and bearers of these cultures to blend, utilizing the indigenous foods of southern Louisiana to create a style of cooking the world knows today as "Creole."

THE AFRICANS: CREOLE AND SOUL

The Africans were landed and bought and sold on as many as three different New Orleans sites. One slave auction was in the ballroom of the elegant St. Charles Hotel. Some say the Africans came with nothing. This is not entirely accurate. They brought with them several things (and some of them tangible) that meant home and life to them. Though when they boarded those dark and dread ships in West Africa and descended into the dank holds, the captives did not know the precise point on the globe to which they were bound, they did know—through rumor—that it was far across the sea. And they had fears that they might not be fed and might, in fact, be

eaten. Against their escape, which they planned, they brought okra seeds, hidden in their hair and ears, for they feared there might be no food at all on the other side. They also brought a knowledge of planting in general. By the 17th century, black West Africans had assembled a formidable food repertory and were cultivating peanuts, eggplant, and corn, probably introduced by the French, who were very active in the slave trade and brought seeds from the New World as well as transporting workers westward. They had also integrated yams, garlic, and onions into their traditional diet of rice, beans, green vegetables, and okra.

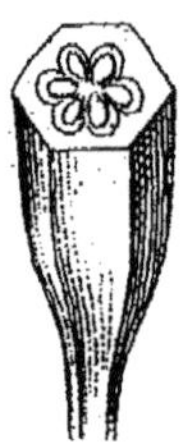

Okra

The popular Lenten Creole soup, gumbo z'herbes, is based on a West African dish. Both Creole and African society have it that a new friend will be found for each green added to this soup. African women were thought of by their owners as cheerful and content, for they seemed always to be singing in the kitchen. This, however, was before clocks were common in plantation kitchens, and the women in fact timed most of their cooking by how long it took to sing certain songs.

As the Africans came from a rice culture, they were not deterred by the swampy New Orleans soil (rice likes water) and were adept at introducing the plant here. The result is that Louisiana has grown into one of our leading rice-producing states.

Slaves were often taken into New Orleans Creole households because of their recognized proficiency in the kitchen. The precise number of dishes they midwifed here is unknown, but the list is definitely long. They had a particular affinity for zesty spices and were shrewd bargainers in the marketplace, often with other Africans. Quite early, New Orleans had become a target for settlement of freed people of color from the Caribbean, who brought with them the food culture of the islands.

Black cooks took the French peasant's thickener, the roux, a step further; they burned it slightly, to make it sweeter, and transformed it into a dark, molasses-like base for many local dishes such as étouffée, gumbo, Creole sauce, and turtle soup. To the roux a cook might add some meat, pork, or fowl too tough to eat on its own, a mélange of herbs, and lots of garlic, and cook the mixture all day into a rich, tangy stew. The tradition survives; today, in New Orleans, a jar of roux made personally by a master cook is considered a nicer gift for a hostess than a box of candy or flowers.

Chef Dookie Chase, an expert on recipes who holds forth at her own restaurant and is the doyenne of Black Creole cooking, maintains, "There isn't one famous 'Creole' dish that didn't pass through the hands of a black cook or chef before it came to be written down," and passed on as Creole. Let us visit Dookie Chase's restaurant and take in her food so that you can taste for yourself.

DOOKIE CHASE

2301 Orleans Ave. (Treme)
Tel. 504/821–2294

The atmosphere is warm, the mood is upbeat. The dining room is colorful with paintings by local and international black artists. The place is often filled with people who seem to know each other and the waiters, and all are having a rollick-

ing good time. A few years back what Dookie served might have been called soul food. The roots of many of these home-style dishes go back more than a century. You must have the panéed veal (lightly breaded and sautéed in butter) or the pork chops cooked with onions. Sausage jambalaya is appropriately stinging, and that immigrant vegetable, okra, is stewed, which eliminates its mucilage (almost). Try it gently on the tongue and let it dissolve there; that's the way to eat it, although pickled, in jars, is even better. Even with the best intentions and technique, however, things do go awry from time to time. Despite all the warmth of the room, the "gumbo thing" was cold. But the sweet potatoes were a revelation, tinged with an intriguing crackling of cooked caramel. There are corn-bread muffins (grainy and uncakelike, which is perfect; muffins should not taste like cake) slathered with butter, and a superb apple pie awaits at the end.

Although hers is the best known, Dookie Chase's is not the only Black Creole restaurant operating in New Orleans. Another, highly recommended and specializing in Southern Creole cooking is:

DUNBAR'S

4927 Freret St. (Uptown)
Tel. 504/899–0734

This is in a tricky neighborhood that's hard to get to, so take a cab; you will be rewarded for your pains in the economy of prices and in the food. Red tufted booths and bright, cheerful paintings compete for attention with stuffed sweet peppers, red beans and rice, very creative and ample seafood po'boys, and mustard greens that you must taste to get to know the real thing. The fried chicken is the best in the world. You're not likely to spend more than $6 for a very generous dinner. Students who can produce a valid ID get iced tea free. It's a wonderful place, perhaps the ideal spot for Sunday supper.

For decades the Baquet family has turned out some of the best home cooking in town. The hard-to-find location is worth the investment in effort for what you will get out of it in value and in the discovery of a real down-home neighborhood eatery.

EDDIE'S RESTAURANT
2119 Law St. (Downtown)
Tel. 504/945–2207

Come for the Thursday night buffet when, for one measly price ($6.95), you get all you can eat of Eddie Baquet's great Creole food and fun as well. There is always some kind of fish or chicken, such as fried catfish with crab and shrimp sauce and oyster dressing. When you think you're finished they load your plate up again. Eddie's is not for the faint-hearted. They like to joke, and they welcome big eaters. Look on Law Street between Frenchmen Avenue and Elysian Fields Avenue.

THE IRISH AND GREAT NEW ORLEANS FOOD

This must be a joke, you say. It must be the Creoles who got that started. When the Irish first came to New Orleans (during the terrible famine in Ireland of the 1840s) in large numbers, there was much discrimination against them. The Creoles kept them out of their neighborhoods and mainly out of their lives. They refused to rent to, to employ, and especially to socialize with the Irish, who were considered a mean, troublesome bunch. The section of the city called the Irish Channel was once an infamous, extremely dangerous Irish slum; it still exists today, though much of it and its shotgun houses (built in the early 1880s) have become gentrified in recent years.

The Creoles also discriminated against the Americans, the New Englanders, Kentuckians, and other Yankees who, after the Purchase, first moved in important numbers into New Orleans, took control of the government, and imposed English as the official language. Americans and Irish were kept out of the Quarter and relegated to no-man's land—across Canal Street from the Quarter (now the Central Business District) and into what is now the Garden District in Uptown.

One thing that brought the two outcast groups together was food. During the 1800s several important Creole restaurants opened. They were meeting places where business was done, especially the Café des Emigrés, and a hangout of Creole bankers; Irish were not welcome. "What do the Irish know or care about food?" was the Creole rejoinder when the Irish complained. But one Irishman dining with Arnaud's founder, Count Arnaud, at his restaurant was different. "I'll show you what the Irish can do," he retorted. "Why, I'll build the finest restaurant in New Orleans, and those fancy French and Creoles will be dying to get in." The immediate Creole response was unrestrained laughter.

But this Irishman's name was Owen Brennan. The result was Brennan's, and the rest is food history. Eventually the Americans and the newly arriving Italians joined in Brennan's effort (they didn't enjoy being scorned either), and today, through judicious management and impeccable taste and service teamed with superior food and ideas, there is more than one restaurant under the Brennan banner. Some of the very best are still under the direction of various members of the Brennan family: Brennan's, Commander's Palace, The Palace Café, and Mister B's.

Ironically, these are all considered Creole restaurants today, for Creole food is what they do in New Orleans. We have already visited Brennan's and stopped briefly at the Palace Café and Mister B's Bistro; the time is ripe now to look more closely at the latter two and take in another: Commander's Palace.

Palace Café

605 Canal Street (CBD)
Tel. 504/523–1661

Here is a big, bustling restaurant in the grand café tradition, with a high ceiling (two levels); many tables; cherry-wood booths; clattering plates; and fast, highly competent, professional service. Everybody feels at home here. What they do is

bistro food, but with a New Orleans Creole twist: crab chops (what are these?—part of the delightful surprise of Creole cuisine), grilled shrimp with fettuccine, rabbit ravioli (of course, influenced by French and especially Italians, who adore rabbit) in piquant sauce. For dessert you can try white chocolate bread pudding. With this bistro food the service is fast. You order, you get; so be prepared. Nevertheless, you should observe the local Creole tradition and eat slowly, savoring every morsel as if it were your last. If the plates pile up by mid-dinner, ask to have the table cleared and demand a fresh tablecloth, a gambit that will earn the respect of the most haughty Creole waiter, wherever it's done, and may slow down the service if things are coming a bit too fast. Then you can sit back with your last glass of wine and watch the late diners stroll into the café; it's a great place to people-watch.

What's a café without oysters, right? The Palace Café has them, too, delivered "fresh from Louisiana's best oyster farmers," they say. The oysters can come lightly dusted and fried; with creamy horseradish sauce; or, for a taste of freshness: Oyster Shooters—a half dozen raw oysters served in individual shot glasses, each in a sauce of cracked black pepper, oil, and lemon. You slug them down one by one to the applause of other customers. These are good for starters, but the oyster pan roast is a Creole oyster extravaganza. This is fresh oysters poached in a rosemary cream sauce topped with Romano cheese and fresh bread crumbs and baked. It comes steaming and hissing to the table, smelling of fragrant hillsides tumbling into the sea. And prices? You get a real break with your oysters at the Café. Not one of the foregoing dishes tops $5.

For a main course there are equal surprises. Dabble with the Creole charcuterie board, an elegant collection of Café-made country pâtés, terrines, and galantines served with Café-made onion bread croutons and a sampling of house-made pickled products and marmalades, all on a wood cutting board that adds a homey touch. As if any were needed.

A treat for the seafarer: Try the Café's seafood gumbo; it's loaded with a Creole combination of filé, salty oysters, shrimp, Gulf fish, peppers, onions, and okra stewed together and served with fluffy south Louisiana rice. It's a great dish for a true taste of the region; the use of filé makes it historically accurate, the way the Indians taught the Europeans.

No matter what you do at the Palace Café, end with the pecan pie—especially if you're not from the South. In mouthfuls crumbly thick with crunchy pecans, you will discover the epitome of pecan taste. It's like eating pralines in a crust—double crunch.

MR. B'S BISTRO

201 Royal St. (French Quarter)
Tel. 504/523-2078

Mr. B's, in an honest, simple format, attempts to revive the distinct styles of regional Louisiana food. To this worthy end, with other restaurants in the Brennan "family," it participates in a statewide program that searches out the best of Louisiana's farm products and regional ingredients, which are organically grown. They are a mainstay of Mr. B's cuisine. Mr. B's is an attractive place, clubby and cozy in style—intimate—

with wood-framed booths and etched glass panels that instantly give you an appetite. I like the line drawing on the menu cover; it shows the place full of patrons in a very relaxed mood. That's the style of the bistro; if not crazy, relaxed. The dress code invites people to come in black tie and jeans.

The menu suggests the same elegant informality. Mr. B's is a bistro; of course there are oysters—fried, spicy, and barbecued. Try the fried catfish fingers. They are crisp, two-bite-size strips of the Louisiana bayou fish that crunch with juicy explosiveness, seasoned with Creole spices and served with a stunning tomato tartar sauce. Also a finger food with a difference are coconut beer shrimp—Louisiana Gulf shrimp, rolled in a beer (our friend Abita) and coconut batter, fried, and served with a Creole marmalade sauce. A fine and exotic taste treat they are.

Gumbo yaya, Mr. B's signature soup, is a classic New Orleans gumbo made with chicken and andouille sausage. In salads and brunch fare, try warm yellowfin tuna salad; the tuna is chunky and rich, the angel hair pasta humid and warm. Then there's a New Orleans double-cut pork chop. It's grilled, thick, and juicy.

Here's a super Creole treat: grilled petit filet mignon with very crisp fried oysters accompanied by wilted (blanched) spinach and hollandaise. No, this is not merely updated surf and turf. The filet is very tender, almost the same texture as the oysters. The tastes, however, are very different and might almost be enough to convince you that beef comes from the sea, or that oysters are fresh from the butcher. Don't be disturbed; it's the way they do things in New Orleans. There are also panée veal and barbecued shrimp, very Creole and containing another delightful surprise. The shrimp are in their shells, New Orleans style, doused with a buttery sauce and served with a roasted whole pepper. All in all, Mr. B's seems up to its self-imposed challenge: sticking with regional specialties and presenting them in a new and inventive way.

The Commander's Palace

1403 Washington Ave. (Garden District)
Tel. 504/899–8221

The Palace is in the Garden District, in the heart of the finest neighborhood in the city. It is not hemmed in or crowded about by other buildings; the only head that rises higher than its Victorian facade is a network of old oaks. Its help, perhaps the finest in the city, is (ironically) drawn from Creole ranks; the food it serves is classic Creole, sometimes updated with American know-how. Here, the $15 prix-fixe lunch is the best deal in town. Ask to be seated in the upstairs

Garden Room and you can enjoy your meal while contemplating the oaks in the courtyard through its window wall. You'll find a wide choice of Creole dishes to choose from: A sauté of shrimp and mushrooms in a garlic butter sauce with wine elegantly pairs foods of almost the same texture and feel in the mouth but with nothing like the same taste—the typical Creole food conceit. The spicy crab cakes in oyster sauce are a sonnet of the sea. Trout crusted with crunchy pecans forms the perfect union; this goes New Orleans's invention of pralines one better. This is the idea: Creoles are never satisfied with one taste in the mouth. At the end, you must have bread pudding soufflé, tops in desserts.

ITALIAN NEW ORLEANS

At the turn of the last century, Italian immigration, as it did elsewhere, hit its peak in New Orleans. By 1890 there were 15,000 Italians living in New Orleans. Many of them, true to their traditions, found their way and a home in the elaborate food culture of the city, where they exerted a profound influence. They moved into the decaying French Quarter, which had been abandoned by the Creoles. The Standard Fruit Company was founded by a New Orleans Italian fruit peddler, Joseph Vaccaro, and a visit to the stands in the French Market or the many ice-cream shops will confirm that Italian culture thrives in the city.

With its warm climate and predominantly Catholic population, New Orleans was an attractive destination for Italian immigration. Many of the Italians who landed at the port of New Orleans came from the island of Sicily. When a massive crop failure took place in Sicily in the Middle Ages, Sicilians had prayed to St. Joseph for relief. The fava bean crop was spared and many Sicilians survived on that and that alone. In thanksgiving, they prepared cooked food and laid it out on an altar for the needy. They brought the celebration with them to New Orleans, it appealed to the local population, and now St. Joseph's Day (March 19, sometimes mid-Lent) is given over to the Italian community to celebrate as their own Mardi Gras. Many New Orleanians of Sicilian descent build altars to St. Joseph in private homes and in the streets of some of the larger Roman Catholic parishes. The altars are festooned with food, and everyone is invited to share in the feast. With the food, St. Joseph medals are also given out, to ward off plague. The Italians also parade through the streets, like the Irish two days earlier, and give out carnations and kisses.

New Orleanians, like everybody else, loved the pastas, pizzas, spicy red sauces, and magical Italian way with the tomato. As soon as they opened, Italian restaurants thrived from the 1890s on.

Bacco

310 Chartres St. (French Quarter)
Tel. 504/522–2426

Here you'll find a half dozen excellent pizzas to assuage your hunger, a dozen or so pastas, Italian roast loin of pork, Tuscan bean soup, and veal dishes that are a talent and a specialty. If you long for a taste of the Italian, this is it. The four dining rooms are stylish in earth tones. They all have silk Venetian chandeliers; one has a vaulted ceiling, another has an Italian street scene mural, and I almost ate the wallpaper in a third.

LA RIVIERA

4506 Shore Dr. (Metairie)
Tel. 504/888-6238

Its signature crab-meat ravioli is so creamy and soft it almost melts in your mouth; you only need to chew the crab. Under a smooth Parmesan sauce, it deserves its partisan following of local Italian Americans. There are also excellent veal dishes (the chop is thick and juicy) served by black-tied waiters in a luxuriously romantic pink room with hand-painted ceiling fans and Italian landscape oil paintings. The service is professional and elegant all by itself. La Riviera is a real Italian night out, the way it's done in a sophisticated Italian city.

IRENE'S CUISINE

539 St. Philip St. (French Quarter)
Tel. 504/529–8811

Strictly speaking, this may not qualify as Italian, but it typifies another way in which the Italian influence is felt in the city's food establishments. Its owner, Irene DiPietro, is from Italy, but her restaurant is strictly New Orleans, using local produce and dishes. Irene's cooking and treatment of these, however, cannot escape her own origins. You must have the garlic and rosemary chicken—an herby sonnet of juices and elusive smoky tastes, it will enter your chicken-of-the-trip sweepstakes at the top of the list. Irene is a believer in freshness and excellence of ingredients. The last time we were here, she ran out of shrimp and excused herself to go and get more. We volunteered to go for her so that she could continue cooking. "No," she said; she had to get them herself from the fisherman—her private source—and she was off to the West Bank, where the shrimp boats come down from the bayous. Maybe we can persuade her to stuff her rosemary chicken with these fabulous shrimp. Among her other achievements are large Gulf prawns stuffed with shrimp, crabmeat, and catfish tails braised with lobster sauce over homemade pasta and marinated grilled pork chops stuffed with Fontina cheese, spinach, and roasted pinenuts glazed with Port wine and mushrooms over white beans. The walls in the tiny restaurant are festooned with snapshots, olive jars, garlic braids, and crockery.

Asians in New Orleans

We can go for a taste of Chinese food without leaving New Orleans culinarily. After the Civil War, when slaves were no longer the only source of workers, and cotton and sugarcane fields were burgeoning, immigration restrictions were relaxed. Asians began arriving in Louisiana to work in the fields. Many remained in the port of New Orleans and there developed a Chinatown, complete with opium dens.

Because the weather was hot and humid in New Orleans, and because it was the style for businessmen to wear starched linen shirts and suits, laundries were a necessity for the male population, and Chinese businesses appeared in every neighborhood. The Chinese also dried shrimp, as they had been doing before they arrived in Louisiana. Many Chinese restaurants sprang up. Their progeny still survive today. In the 1950s and 1960s many Japanese, Vietnamese, Korean, and other Asians arrived, with similar restaurant results.

KUNG'S DYNASTY

1912 St. Charles Ave. (Garden District) or
Riverwalk, at Poydras St. and Mississippi River
Tel. 504/525–6669

This is a dynasty of two restaurants run by the Kung family. Both offer reliable Chinese mainstays localized with Louisiana ingredients. Wonton is larded with crab meat; fiery Szechuan sauce inflames stir-fried oysters; mu-shu pork comes with outstanding crepes. Try the five-flavor shrimp as an appetizer. If you want the taste of a Chinatown you know, try the festive Peking duck. The Garden District branch of this mini chain has the nicer decor.

SAMURAI SUSHI

609 Decatur St. (French Quarter)
Tel. 504/525–9595

A quiet little pop-in place only a block from Jackson Square, it's very convenient for some lighter New Orleans fare with a Japanese accent. The extensive selection at the small sushi bar runs the gamut of local fish. There are vegetarian entrées, too. The interior is mostly red carpet and gray marble. It's a hangout for the Greens (ecology advocates) of the town.

NINJA

8115 Jeannette St. (Uptown)
Tel. 504/866–1119

A Japanese landing if you're tired of sybaritic Creole and Cajun: Here you'll find Japanese home cooking. Sukiyaki, tempura, donburi, and sushi are all served in a traditional setting of earth tones with gray trim. The sushi bar is finished in oak, and the walls are covered with Japanese photo scenes.

Ghenghis Khan

4053 Tulane Ave. (Treme)
Tel. 504/482–4044

Korean food is often surprisingly spicy, and this style finds a home on the New Orleanian palate. Ask for *bul goki,* or "fire beef," perhaps the Korean national dish—it's beef marinated in sesame oil, garlic, hot chili peppers, a dash of vinegar, and some sugar. Korea has pastures for grazing, so, unlike most Asians, Koreans eat a significant amount of beef. Try also hot pot *chon gol* (vegetables, shrimp, and beef heated in a stone vessel and served over rice). For a taste of the exotic, try whole baby octopus; another Korean specialty, it is very salty, like the sea or strong-flavored oysters. Tenderized with cross cuts, it is generally stewed and served sliced; watch out for the suction cups. All this is accompanied nightly by live classical music.

CARNIVAL, MARDI GRAS, AND OTHER CELEBRATIONS

CARNIVAL AND MARDI GRAS

On the Christian church calendar, Shrove Tuesday or, in French, **Mardi Gras** (Fat Tuesday), precedes Ash Wednesday and is the last day for any sort of indulgence before the 40-day Lenten stint of self-denial and fasting. In New Orleans, the weeks just prior to Lent—Carnival—are marked by celebrations and unfettered feasting, culminating with the outrageous Mardi Gras Day itself—the final 24 hours during which New Orleanians can partake of the foods and participate in the lifestyle they so enjoy before settling into grim austerity until Easter liberates them.

In New Orleans and its vicinity there are several celebrations and foods that mark this tradition, which started here when French Québec-born explorer Sieur d'Iberville (Pierre Le Moyne), his brother Sieur de Bienville (Jean Baptiste Le Moyne), and their crew camped on a spit of sand on the Mississippi River. They sailed on to what is now New Orleans, arriving on March 2, 1699 (March 3 was Mardi Gras that year). They named the place Pointe du Mardi Gras, and it wasn't long before the French who settled New Orleans began to celebrate the day.

The tradition survived through settlements of Spanish, Irish, Italians, and even Yankees to continue right up to this day.

A month or two before Shrove Tuesday, Mardi Gras preparations begin. On January 6, Christmas decorations come down throughout the town and traditional Mardi Gras colors—purple (justice), green (faith), and gold (power)—go up. The period of Carnival has officially begun. Carnival is a Latin term meaning farewell to the flesh; however, most carnival celebrants strive to make its memory last. The parties spill into the streets, and there are continual parades the two weekends just prior to the mammoth explosion that is Mardi Gras Day.

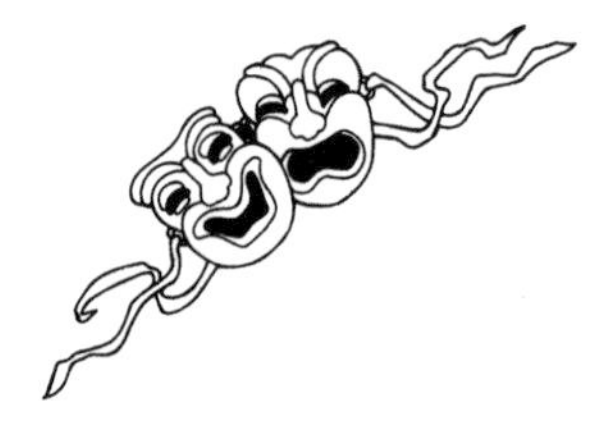

The parades go on day and night over four main routes (listed in the *Times-Picayune*). Night is suspended in the reflected glow of fireworks, and the background din of celebration is constant. To the casual observer everything appears to be in chaos, but nothing is casual. It's organized with the precision of a military armored assault. The more than 350 floats roll on flatbeds that would credit a Rose Bowl; the day comes together as the result of long planning, tradition, and hard work. Mardi Gras may have its origins as a religious feast, but today the whole town pitches in to create a holiday that is gigantically American. It's a combination of Ringling Brothers and Barnum & Bailey coming down Main Street, V-E Day, and New Year's Eve in Times Square.

Absolutely fundamental to Mardi Gras are the 60 or so parades of the krewes between January 6th and Ash Wednesday. Krewes are secret marching societies; members all wear masks in the parades and, in this elitist little world, it's taboo to discuss members' identities and krewe details. They were established to put on Mardi Gras events and compete with one another to present the biggest, splashiest, and most exciting parades, balls, and other galas.

The biggest parade is that of the Krewe of Endymion, which always marches on Saturday. It bills itself as the largest nonmilitary parade in the world, and continues to make good on its motto, "Throw 'til it hurts," as its member marchers and float riders toss favors (plastic cups with their insignias/parade themes on them, multicolor "gold" doubloons, and beads) to the crowd. The second largest is the Krewe of Bacchus parade (you see what these groups celebrate) on Sunday. Together, all the krewes have an estimated combined membership of 2,300, and each year they toss to bystanders some 1½ million cups, 2½ million doubloons (specially made up by a favor company in France), and 200,000 gross of beads. If the effect is epic, the price is monumental. The total cost of a krewe ball and parade has reached a million dollars. One of the exotically decorated floats can cost $100,000 to build. The marching organizations pay for their parades and ensuing balls by tithing their members (as little as $100, as much as thousands) for the privilege of participating. The parades are a gift to the people of the city and its guests; and the balls are private parties for the entertainment of friends and krewe members.

If you want to politic for an invitation to a ball and/or to march, it's possible. The leading organizations to approach are: Endymion, Bacchus, The Mystic Krewe of Cosmos, Momus, The Original Illinois Club, Proteus, Rex, Zeus, and Zulu. Inquiries should be made to: Germaine Wells Mardi Gras Museum (813 Bienville St., New Orleans, LA 70112). But be careful; the initiation fee for new members can be as much as

$1,000. If you just want to go to the ball and have a good vantage point for watching the parade, you may pay less. What do you get for your money? Selected kings and queens reign at the balls and ride the floats of major krewes. Show business celebrities often do the honors. Entertainers like Pete Fountain and Doc Severinsen are usually tapped to play for krewe members and their friends at the balls. Typically, the outrageously decorated flatbeds of a larger, wealthier krewe roll along among nearly 15,000 fantastically costumed marchers. You may see Energizer rabbits, dancing condoms, Nubian royalty, Oscar Wilde, the Romantic poets, and perhaps French revolutionaries leading a transvestite Marie Antoinette to the guillotine amid troops of countless clowns and fools.

Members of the black community have their own krewes and many march as Indians. There are the Wild Magnolias, the Black Eagles, the Yellow Pocahontases, and the Wild Squatoolas. Some are in enormous, fanciful headdresses, purple, with caged birds mounted in the feathers, others in bizarre costumes featuring seashell breastplates. These tribes of Mardi Gras Indians have the most colorful costumes seen this side of the Ziegfeld Follies. The motif of Indians may be a tribute; many runaway slaves were taken in by the Indian tribes, where they intermarried and joined in tribal life.

On Mardi Gras Day the parades are followed up by the sanitation department with its water trucks, sweepers, and blowers. By midnight, the six-block-long party along Bourbon Street winds down, and police with bull horns holler, "Mardi Gras is over," and sweep the crowd forward. But some dazed and bleary fun-seekers, sloshing with beer and good humor, still line the wrought-iron balconies above, willing to shimmy a passerby for a throw of some beads. Desultory music floats with debris in the streets. It's over. Still, you've got to eat. Who can face seclusion and sadness on an empty stomach?

The food that is de rigueur during Carnival is king cake. It is a *Pithiviers,* a large, round puff pastry cake with almond paste filling. The king of France (Louis XV himself) started the tradition that survives to this day when he gave the queen a piece of his cake with a bean inside—doubtless suggestive of fertility. But, alas, a real Pithiviers is something very hard to make. It is practically all butter and sugar; the flour is only for binding, and in the New Orleans heat and humidity, it is nearly impossible to handle. You roll and you roll, and the dough breaks and breaks; and the more you roll the stickier the mass becomes. So, many people give up on tradition and

use a coffee ring or a brioche ring. Others keep a slab of marble in the refrigerator for pastry and roll away on that. One of the places in New Orleans where you can get a legitimate king cake, a real Pithiviers—the most delicious pastry in the world—is luckily right in the French Quarter.

CROISSANT D'OR PATISSERIE

617 Ursulines St. (French Quarter)

Tel. 504/524–4663

This is the New Orleans headquarters for French pastries—always made on the premises. It is also an adorable coffeehouse, so you can sit and enjoy French croissants, brioches, and tarts that are as good as if you were in Paris, or even better. In good weather, find a table in the lovely courtyard, which has a gurgling fountain.

New Orleans office workers often observe the feasting of Carnival between the Feast of the Epiphany (January 6) and Mardi Gras Day with king cakes. Each round cake, decorated with sprinkles of granulated sugar in the official Carnival colors—purple, green, and gold—contains a small plastic baby Jesus (sometimes the baby is white, sometimes black, and sometimes mulatto). Whoever gets the piece containing the

baby has to buy the next king cake. For Mardi Gras celebrants, the stakes are higher: each king cake contains a tiny bean or plastic baby or gilt paper crown, and whoever gets the piece with the bean, baby, or crown inside is "king" of Mardi Gras Day and has to take everyone to dinner. If you get it, however, you can do what millions do; swallow the bean whole, palm it, or secrete it inside an enemy's slice. On Mardi Gras Day, there are many more king cakes devoured in New Orleans than there are kings crowned. If, however, the king decides to be a sport about it, he or she (in case there's a queen declared) must move swiftly to put a dinner in place. King, queen, and guests must be at table before midnight. Tomorrow starts Lent—and the 40 days of fasting.

Many enjoy on Mardi Gras night what will be forgone in the 40 days ahead. Chiefly this is flesh. Roasts, ribs of beef, and "just a good steak" are very popular fare for Mardi Gras night. As a city, New Orleans offers an accommodating selection:

THE RIB ROOM

Royal Orleans Hotel
621 St. Louis St. (French Quarter)
Tel. 504/529–7045

This place may make you feel like a feudal potentate dining on meat in medieval splendor. The rustic dining room with exposed brick and chandeliers is filled with rotisseries with huge roasts turning on spits. The rib they put before you covers a whole plate and is crusty with char and succulent juices.

RUTH'S CHRIS STEAKHOUSE

711 N. Broad St. (Mid-City)
Tel. 504/486–0810 or 504/888–3600 (Metairie)

Here you'll indulge in upscale formal dining, surrounded by oil paintings on the walls and a black, red, and wine color scheme. If you don't mind cholesterol (just once in a while), this meal's for you. Only well-aged slabs of prime beef—plump fillets (higher than they are long) or porterhouse—are served with butter sizzling on top. The string-cut french fries sop up the juices and are a meal in themselves. After this you may feel that a diet of 40 days is in order.

Still, if you want to overdo, New Orleans is the place, any day of the week, especially during Carnival:

Lundi Gras. On the Monday (*lundi* in French) before Mardi Gras, as the festivities are reaching a feverish peak, the

kings of the major krewes of Zulu and Rex arrive in the Spanish Plaza among general pandemonium. A free concert and fireworks follow when the sun goes down. It's a fitting appetizer to the final feast of Mardi Gras Day.

Courir de Mardi Gras. There's a place upcountry where the folks do more with Mardi Gras than watch parades. In French, Courir de Mardi Gras means "Mardi Gras Run," and that's what it is. Troops of Cajuns race through the flatlands just north of Lafayette on horseback. Fences, fallen trees, and streams present no serious barriers. It's the Cajun counterpart

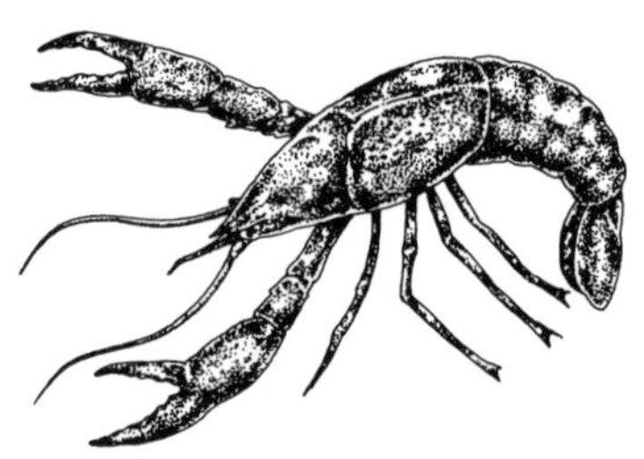

to riding to hounds, but they do it for food, as they ride from participating household to household, rounding up the ingredients for the fabulous Mardi Gras gumbo, which is both the object and reward of the Cajun hunt.

If you're collecting food for a gumbo, you've got to have crawfish. Fifteen-year-old Danielle Mizeaux's foot sinks to the ankle in the mud below the floating green film of duckweed on a bayou just outside Livonia. But Danielle is all Cajun. She pulls her foot up with a suctioning slurp and plods on down the bayou. A plastic washtub tethered to her middle trails behind her as she visits her string of crawfish traps marked with fish floats. Retrieving a trap, she dumps its contents into the tub, an operation she hopes is uneventful. One of the traps the week before had a water moccasin in it. She dropped the trap fast, and the snake swam away just as fast, but it gave her a start. Danielle has been trapping and selling crawfish down on the state road through town for nearly a year, a pastime that keeps her occupied and in pin money. "It's better than babysitting," she'll tell you, and her hours are her own. Besides, like most Cajuns, she enjoys the beauty and quiet of the swamp; there's nothing better than being up to your hips in nature. It's Lundi Gras today, however, so the string of traps she has to gather contain crawfish destined for the Mardi Gras gumbo or

boil instead of for her own private enterprise. The following day, the riders come by to snatch up the basket of crawfish.

Another thing you've got to have for gumbo is a chicken. Back in the town, the riders dismount at a small house and barnyard at the end of a dusty dirt road. The woman of the house here has promised them a chicken for the gumbo pot and is stroking it. But according to the rules of the game, nothing should come too easy. "You've got to catch it," she says, and throws it at the captain of the hunt. He misses. The chicken seems to know what's up. She flies. The captain is after her, and so are all the riders. The chicken has her mind set on not being caught, but the Cajuns are just as determined to catch it. The barnyard is a scramble of flying feathers and head knocking, more dangerous than a parade. Presently, though, the bird is cornered. She defends herself with beak and sharp talons. Few will stoop to pick her up. "Tough bird," judges the hunt captain. The rest of the Cajuns all fall down laughing. Persistence prevails, however, the chicken runs into a sitting hunter and is bagged, hissing and clucking.

The hunt is far from over, though. You still need a pig for the gumbo, for the ribs that go with it. But you don't want to make the hunt too easy. So the pig is greased and chased

around a bit before the riders come. It takes the better part of the afternoon to catch him. By the time this is done, Danielle has her crawfish, the hunters their chicken and pig, and the better part of the Mardi Gras gumbo is gathered up. Everyone repairs to the household with the biggest pot to partake. The gumbo is cooked according to Cajun tradition—thick, dark roux, flavorful, spicy soup with lots of vegetables and crawfish, with ribs served on the side. Meanwhile, a fiddler fiddles and those who were riding dance.

It is widely asserted that the holy trinity of New Orleans (both Creole and Cajun) cooking is: garlic (a few cloves cut up), finely chopped onion, and bell pepper (cut up). These are simmered in a pan with olive oil and stirred until the onion is translucent; a great many dishes begin this way. The holy trinity is the base of almost everything you need to season. On it you can add a variety of things. A few tomatoes, cored, seeded, and quartered, are added; the pan is covered and allowed to simmer slowly for 15 minutes. When you uncover the pan, stir the contents, and you've got a spaghetti sauce as good as any your grandma simmered all day in the pot. This sauce, with so much personality, will go well with any number of things—pork chops, a nice flounder (adding some taste to that flaky fish). But I like it best with shrimp and tortellini. Do it the

New Orleans way, however: First sauté the shrimp in hot butter with their shells on. Then turn them into the sauce and eat them in their shells. They're delicious, thin, crunchy—and very good for you, too. They also provide a pleasing contrast to the softness of the tortellini.

A Courir de Mardi Gras Festival that welcomes visitors takes place at Church Point, Louisiana, in Acadia Parish, just a few miles north of Lafayette. Contact Church Point Chamber of Commerce (Box 218, Church Point, LA 70525, tel. 318/684–3030). Alternatively, you can repair to Enola's Cajun Café in Carencro (*see* Chapter 9) for a gumbo that is authentic and a welcome that is warm.

Still in the vicinity, there's another restaurant we could recommend that expresses the soul of Mardi Gras, where you can get up and dance if you wish.

MULATE'S

325 Mill Ave.
Breaux Bridge, LA 70517
Tel. 318/332–4648 or 800/422–2586

This is a very famous Cajun rendezvous. If you're not having gumbo (Mulate's does not put crawfish in their gumbo), you must have their seafood platter: stuffed crab, fried shrimp, fried oysters, jambalaya, stuffed bell peppers, and frogs' legs. There is live zydeco music seven nights a week. Cypress beams hold up the dance floor. Cajun art and festive posters reflecting Cajun history decorate the walls.

If you can't visit New Orleans during Mardi Gras, stop by the Germaine Wells Mardi Gras Museum or visit Blaine Kern's Mardi Gras World. A visit to the Mardi Gras Center or Serendipitous Masks may just enable you to take some of Mardi Gras home.

The first name in Mardi Gras magic stands on the other side of the Mississippi River in Algiers. Cross on the ferry that leaves from the foot of Canal Street—a nice way to see the river and enjoy its breezes.

BLAINE KERN'S MARDI GRAS WORLD

233 Newton St. (Algiers)
Tel. 504/361–7821

Take the van that meets the ferry and shuttles visitors to Mardi Gras World; the ride costs nothing, and the alternative walk is down several long, lonely blocks. Blaine Kern has long been the leading artist and creator of Mardi Gras floats. His is the largest float-building firm in the world, and his creations are mind-boggling and fanciful. Imagine the mammoth radiance of a giant sunburst floating at second-story level pulling a tap-dancing jazz band. A tour here takes you through warehouses, workshops, and crypts and into the heart of the stagecraft. It's like visiting the backstage bowels of an opera house. Kern has made floats for 40 Mardi Gras; wait till you see the masks. Visitors to the sanctorum watch artists and builders at work, view a film about the craft of Mardi Gras, and buy Carnival memorabilia (there are some terrific items in the gift shop). A photo of yourself alongside one of the gigantic, fanciful parade creations makes the perfect Mardi Gras souvenir, even if you weren't there. It is a great place to take children. Blaine Kern himself often conducts tours through the unique facility. He is an excellent source of restaurant tips. (Admission, $4.50 adults, $2.50 children. Open daily 9:30–4:30, except the 2 weeks before Mardi Gras Day.)

MARDI GRAS CENTER

831 Chartres St. (French Quarter)
Tel. 504/524–4384

If you're nursing a crush on Carnival and its artifacts, come here. Masks worn at Mardi Gras are popular as gifts. They are also perfect mementos or decorative pieces for the home. You should be aware they don't come cheap; the better ones are hand-crafted, locally made, and bear the artist's signature. A nice ceramic or feather mask starts at only about $10, but they can go up to about $300, depending on materials and workmanship. The center is where many New Orleanians go for custom-made masks, costumes (some of these are stunning—like those of commedia dell'arte) and sundry accessories. The center has a large stock with hundreds of masks, including animal masks. Centrally located, it is a good place to browse on your way to or from lunch.

Serendipitous Masks
831 Decatur St.
Tel. 504/522–9152

Here you'll find an excellent stock of feather masks and ornate Mardi Gras headdresses. It's no accident; the artists are on the premises. Masks are made to order in very little time.

OTHER CELEBRATIONS

The closing of Mardi Gras day does not close off our explorations of religious/national-origin-based celebrations and parades in New Orleans. Two more, like Mardi Gras, are closely identified with ethnic groups that influenced the development of the city—in this case, the Irish and the Italians.

Everywhere in the world, it seems, when March 17 rolls around, there's a **St. Patrick's Day parade.** I've seen them in Paris, Puerto Rico, New York, Boston, and Dublin—and New Orleans has one, too. It doesn't necessarily come on March 17 on the nose, however; sometimes it's the weekend before, sometimes the week after. Again, consult the *Times-Picayune,* your hotel concierge, or the Convention and Visitors Bureau. Everybody in town dons green and comes down to the parade. The float riders throw favors to the crowds, as well as recycled (from Mardi Gras Day) doubloons and beads. Led by such groups as Joe's Jingle Marching Club, the Kazoozies Floozies, the Pipes and Drums of New Orleans, and Pete Fountain's Half-Fast Walking Club, the parade moves through the French Quarter headed Uptown (to the Irish Channel), with several stops:

Molly's at the Market Pub
1107 Decatur St. (French Quarter)
Tel. 504/525–5169

The parade steps off from here. Most beer at local pubs this day is green; you can find a correctly colored brew at Molly's.

O'FLAHERTY'S IRISH CHANNEL PUB

514 Toulouse St. (French Quarter)
Tel. 504/529–1317

On this day this place immerses you in Irish heritage. They offer, with your beer, live concerts of Irish singing, and ceili dancing accompanied by the fiddle, the flute, and the whistle (Chieftains-style).

PAT O'BRIEN'S BAR

718 St. Peter St. (French Quarter)
Tel. 504/525–4823

It's St. Patrick's Day, so of course you've got to drink lunch. This is one of the most popular spots in town to do it. What they are known for is the Pat O'Brien's Hurricane, a sweet, highly alcoholic, mixed rum and fruit drink served in a tall, hurricane-lantern-shape glass (which you can keep; you have to put a deposit down on the glass when you pay for your drink; if you bring the glass back in one piece, you get your deposit back). You can sip away in a beautiful backyard patio, a smaller interior bar, or a medium-size piano bar to the sounds of a terrific piano or take your drink, to go, next door to:

PRESERVATION HALL

726 St. Peter St. (French Quarter)
Tel. 504/522–2841

The Hall is interesting architecturally and is a living museum of strictly classic New Orleans jazz. Standing room only, it's a great way to finish a parade, a day, and yourself.

Another, and perhaps the number-one place the crowd breaks up to go to is appropriately in the middle of the city's Irish Channel, Uptown.

PARASOL'S BAR AND RESTAURANT

2533 Constance St. (Uptown)
Tel. 504/897–5413 or 504/899–2054

Here the green-beer crowd congregates; and here you can get a sip, too. Many of the paraders stand outside to drink. Step inside and you'll know why so many are outside—the place is seriously dingy. But it's worth the fight to the bar for a space: It's to Parasol's that native New Orleanians will take you for what they maintain are the best po'boys in town. Roast beef is traditional on St. Pat's, but the oyster one is very good, too.

Another likely spot for good and cheap proletarian grub on a holiday is not so far away:

MOTHER'S

401 Poydras St. (CBD)
Tel. 504/523–9656

For the blue-collar crowd here, the gimmick is four kinds of jambalayas—sausage, chicken, ham, or shellfish—served on a fluffy bed of rice. Eat 'em with the home-style biscuits. Just pick your favorite and go with it, and go home a jambalaya expert. Founded in 1938, the bar has lots of wood and exposed brick.

Almost directly after St. Patrick comes St. Joseph: **St. Joseph's Day** (March 19) is a big event in New Orleans. St. Joseph is especially honored by the city's large and influential Sicilian population. In the Middle Ages, when famine threatened Sicily, Sicilians prayed to St. Joseph, the patron saint of families, for deliverance. One crop didn't fail—the fava bean—and Sicily pulled through. In thanksgiving, the Sicilians, knowing what hunger was, laid cooked food on altars for the needy. These altars became known as St. Joseph's Day altars, and the event has since been observed every year on the saint's feast day. Can New Orleans's Italians do any less? New Orleanians of Sicilian and/or Italian descent commemorate the date in the same way. Throughout the year many of them make vows that if a prayer for such and such is answered, they will build an altar to St. Joseph in their home each year on his feast day.

By the looks of things, a good number of prayers have been answered. The day of St. Joseph dawns in an explosion of thanks and faith. The altars are almost baroquely decorated with bread baked in the shape of wreaths, crosses, and hearts. Italian cakes and other *dolci* (sweets) are decorated with praying hands and bibles. Baskets of fava beans and St. Joseph's medals (good for warding off the plague) are distributed to visitors to keep away hunger in the coming year. No meats are placed on these altars, in keeping with the Lenten observance, but there are dishes of *baccalà* (codfish), stuffed crabs, mounds of crawfish, eggplant in olive oil, artichokes, many other vegetables, fruits, pastas in all imaginable shapes, and pasta sculptures, too. These days, the food is set out on special St. Joseph altars around the city, including a huge one in the Spanish Plaza, open for viewing and sampling. If you wish to go, check the *Times-Picayune* classified section for invitations to feasts at St. Joseph altars in homes, churches, and businesses.

ST. JOSEPH'S CHURCH

1802 Tulane Ave. (Uptown)
Tel. 504/522–3186

This church sets up one of the largest outdoor altars in the world. Be sure to bring your camera. On St. Joseph's Day, children dress up as Mary and Joseph to commemorate the Holy Family's search for shelter in Bethlehem. An elaborate Italian feast is prepared, displayed, and then served to the poor of the neighborhood.

On St. Joseph's Night, the Italian community parades through the French Quarter. It has all the festive aspects of a giant block party, with floats (each depicting a different Italian province), horses, playing bands—you'll swear you're in Sicily —and marchers, members of Italian-American social clubs. Paraders trade red, white, and green carnations for kisses and throw fava beans to the crowd.

Another arresting aspect of this St. Joseph's parade is that the black community joins in; they parade as Mardi Gras Indians. It's something worth seeing—only twice a year, on Mardi Gras Day and on St. Joseph's Night, do these spectacular strutters appear in their dazzling, fantastically imaginative costumes. The exceptional appearance of the Mardi Gras "tribes" on this particular feast day may have to do with the ancient veneration of St. Joseph in voodoo rituals.

Several more groups of people that have come to live in New Orleans periodically celebrate their origins with outbursts of their cultures, giving other New Orleanians, and you, a chance to explore their musical and culinary traditions.

Black Heritage Festival

Audubon Zoo, Box 4327
New Orleans, LA 70178
Tel. 504/861–2537

Write or call to fine-tune the details. The zoo, one of the largest in the South and a world-class facility, hosts several ethnic celebrations in the embrace of its beautiful and parklike surroundings. This one takes place in the first half of March. It includes gospel and jazz performances, art exhibits, paintings for sale, and ethnic food. There is plenty here that you may never have seen in your hometown, and you risk getting something good to eat.

NEW ORLEANS JAZZ AND HERITAGE FESTIVAL

1205 N. Rampart St.
New Orleans, LA 70116
Tel. 504/522–4786

This high-energy event, gathering more than 4,000 musicians to jam, takes place at the fairgrounds in Mid-City and at night in concert spaces (including riverboats) around town. The food is good, but you can hardly hear yourself eat. The Jazz Fest is held over the last weekend in April and the first in May; so popular has it become that one weekend can't hold

the crowds. Performers include internationally known jazz artists—the Neville Brothers, Dr. John, and Wynton Marsalis have performed here. It welcomes gospel choirs (Mahalia Jackson has sung here), Cajun and zydeco bands, rhythm and blues bands, and sounds in between. Tickets for the Jazz Fest nighttime concerts sell quickly; be sure to order well ahead, as early as mid-February. You can book and get information in advance from TicketMaster (tel. 800/488–5252).

The crowds are mammoth, the fairgrounds soft infield. If there is even a hint of rain, be sure to wear good rubber boots or you'll squish your leather shoes in the mud. If it's sunny, wear a hat, sunscreen, and a long-sleeve shirt for sun protection. Don't forget you are very far south. If you're seriously into learning about food, the Jazz Festival is a must (try to gear your visit to New Orleans to its schedule); cooking demonstrations (they can't do anything in the food capital without food) range from the basic to the stunning and illuminate just about every food technique described in this book. Two stages on the grounds hold cooking demos and presentations; here is a sampling of their offerings to whet your appetite. Some of the events take place simultaneously (call for schedules).

Once you're on the fairgrounds, find the Food Heritage Stage, the hot spot for those who love good food. It's an intimate indoor setting where both legendary chefs and down-home cooks prepare Creole, Cajun, African-American, Southern, and Native American dishes.

The outdoor Louisiana Camp Shack stage offers demonstrations on "How Men Cook," including obligatory, daily at 2 PM, seafood boils. It's only somewhat like a New England clambake; you must see this to learn how it's done. A classic Louisiana kitchen garden growing a variety of Southern vegetables and herbs sets the stage for further cooking demonstrations.

Food events during a typical Jazz Fest weekend may include:

- An alligator-skinning demonstration with gator farmers and ranchers who tell tall swamp tales and serve up the critter in a variety of tempting ways.
- Chef George Rhode of Straya Restaurant preparing an updated Cajun classic—Shrimp Corn Maque Choux Pasta, with New Orleans sauce and explanations.
- Chefs Pamela Neyrey and Richard Stewart of the Gumbo Shop demonstrating the making of king cake and discoursing on the history of this interesting Mardi Gras tradition.
- Pete Giovenco of Deer Meat Processing, an expert on dressing wild game, preparing his famous duck sausage in the old charcuterie style.

- The executive chef at the Commander's Palace, preparing and explaining one of the Commander's signature dishes, and you get a chance to ask questions.
- A discussion and demonstration by the Louisiana Cooperative Extension Service on techniques for container-grown vegetables.
- Lucy Mike King, Louisiana's "Strawberry Ambassador," sharing some of her secret strawberry recipes.
- Frank Brigtsen of Brigtsen's Restaurant demonstrating New Orleans foods in general and sharing his individual blend of culinary magic in preparing red beans and rice.
- Janie Luster of the United Houma Nation presenting some of the significant contributions of Native Americans to New Orleans and Louisiana food. The all-day demonstration includes fresh filé gumbo, smothered crabs prepared in the Houma tradition, and an array of food preservation techniques, including traditional corn grinding and salting shrimp. Houma Fancy Dancers may also perform.

There are 66 booths in all demonstrating and promoting foods, plus the informative stage demonstrations. You'll find crawfish served in 17 different ways, suckling pig, fried soft-shell crabs, stuffed shrimp, catfish, barbecue alligator with fried green tomatoes, pralines, sweet potato pone, and more to tempt your palate, while rhythm and blues, zydeco, marching bands, and jazz riffs tingle your ears.

Honduran Independence Day Festival

c/o The Honduran Foundation
3001 Roberta St., Metairie 70003
Tel. 504/528–3950

In the second week of September, this festival fills the French Market air with the aromas of tacos and empanadas and the music of Honduran bands. For this free ethnic food fair, Honduran hotels send staff from Honduras to prepare Central American fare such as *carne asada* (roast meat), tacos, tamales, *yuca con chicharrón* (cassava with pork cracklings), and empanadas. There are exhibits of Honduran art, as well as folkloric dances and live bands.

THE GREEK FESTIVAL

Hellenic Cultural Center
1200 Robert E. Lee Blvd., 70122
Tel. 504/282–0259

On Memorial Day weekend, 11,000 people fill the huge festival gym and outdoor tents; these overflow with Greek music, crafts, and food. The entrance fee, $2, includes a chance to win two round-trip tickets to Greece—and to get a crack at the food. There are gyros, roasted lamb on spits, Greek salad, and pastries of all kinds against a backdrop of Greek dancers. It's the place in New Orleans for ouzo and baklava.

THE LOUISIANA SWAMP FESTIVAL

Audubon Zoo
Box 4327, New Orleans 70178
Tel. 504/861–2537

This festival in mid-October is a four-day salute to Louisiana Bayou Country, with swamp exhibits, Cajun food, dancing, and music. You can even shake hands with a live swamp animal. You can sample foods such as fried gator, gumbo, crawfish étouffée, smoked duck, and shrimp bread. There is Cajun and zydeco music from around the state, handcrafted arts, Cajun dancing, and Cajun storytelling.

Oktoberfest

Deutsches Haus
200 S. Galvez St., 70119 (CBD)
Tel. 504/522–8014, 504/834–4146

On Saturdays and Sundays from the last weekend in September through the third weekend in October, Germans celebrate their long New Orleans history. They eat bratwurst, knockwurst, sauerbraten, and other German specialties; drink imported beers, as well as Abita and Dixie; and dance to *Hofkatelle* (palace) bands at the Deutsches Haus (normally open only Wednesday, Thursday, and Friday); and you can, too.

FOOD FAIRS AND FESTIVALS

In the capital of food there are celebrations of food. Each year a variety of festivals proclaim and worship certain edibles that have filtered down the Mississippi or Gulf shoreline from Cajun country, plantations, reef trawlers, and the depths of tradition. There are samples, treats, recipes, and a mighty good time to be had if you go.

NEW ORLEANS

A NEW ORLEANS CHRISTMAS

December 1–31

Tel. 800/673–5725

This monthlong celebration of holiday activities includes tours of historic antebellum homes dressed in 19th-century holiday finery, candlelight caroling in Jackson Square, choirs and tree lightings, fireworks along the river, holiday cooking demonstrations by famous chefs, and *réveillons* (Christmas revels) menus served in 17 participating restaurants recreating 1800s dinners, many of which include game. A Celtic Christmas week with madrigals is celebrated at an Irish pub. Some of the top restaurants in the city offer holiday dinners that include a minimum of four courses and free *café brûlot,* priced from $17.95 to $38; you have only to take your choice. There's a *bûche de Noël* (Yule log cake) demonstration at La Madeleine French Bakery and Café. Ask for the special Papa Noël hotel rates, which are in effect the entire month and start as low as $45 double occupancy.

Christmas visitors to the Crescent City can step back into old New Orleans tradition as well as the spirit of Christmases past in the Vieux Carré. Creole families of the 19th century attended midnight mass at beautiful St. Louis Cathedral, then returned home for the réveillon dinner, which consisted of eggs, fish, fowl, meat, sweetbreads, and the Creole specialty, *daube glacé* (well-seasoned beef brisket). The meal was replete with eggnog, pastries, meringues, and crystallized fruits, and it

often ended with a jelly-filled cake dripping with rum and whipped cream. Today's réveillon, adapted from this menu, is offered at 17 top New Orleans restaurants such as Arnaud's and Galatoire's.

In addition to classic dining, A New Orleans Christmas offers a variety of classic activities: Trips to view the traditional bonfires along the Mississippi that light the way to the city for Papa Noël, as well as performances of *The Nutcracker* and *The Red Shoes.*

FRENCH QUARTER FESTIVAL

Early April
c/o Sandra Dartus, 100 Conti St.
New Orleans, LA 70130
Tel. 504/522–5730

A mammoth event, it draws about 250,000 people each year to the area from Bourbon Street to the river. Food and music (more than 100 hours of performances) are the joint focuses of the festival; some of the musical groups are well known and some of the restaurants are big name. The restaurants set up booths throughout the fair, where interesting staples of the region may be tasted: alligator sauce piquant, crawfish in lobster sauce, *boudin* (sausage), crawfish pies, jambalaya, gumbo, crawfish chili, alligator sausage, muffulettas, mustard greens and grilled chicken, eggplant dressing, cheesecake with praline sauce, shrimp po'boys, red beans and rice, bread pudding, and other Creole/Cajun favorites are offered either free or at a nominal ($3) cost at the booths. The World's Largest Jazz Brunch, set up at Jackson Square and Woldenberg Park, opens Friday noon and goes to 8 PM; there's also the World's Largest Praline Contest (you guess the weight) and tasting.

FRENCH MARKET TOMATO FESTIVAL

New Orleans, early June
c/o Bridget Turner
Tel. 504/522–2621

Held in the French Market, this small festival (it draws about 50,000 people) focuses chiefly on the famous, fabulous, and sumptuous Creole tomato. Not a specific botanical category, the Creole tomato is the result of good growing conditions; it gets its assets—sweetness and size—from the rich Louisiana earth, plenty of rainfall, and a hot Southern sun. It is thin skinned and very delicate, so it doesn't travel well. At the Tomato Festival booths offer such dishes as Cajun stuffed tomato, tomato and basil salad, tomato po'boys, as well as famous Creole dishes that depend on tomatoes—shrimp Creole, Creole sauce, jambalaya, and so on. Local chefs demonstrate tomato techniques and live music gets your feet marching.

New Orleans Food and Wine Experience

New Orleans, mid-July
Box 70514
New Orleans, LA 70172
Tel. 504/529–9463

Here is something to sharpen connoisseurship; under the direction of Mary Ann Stierwald, sommelier at Brennan's, 150 wines from near (Ponchartrain Vineyards) and far (around the world) are matched with New Orleans foods from 80 restaurants. Thursday there are 15 vintner dinners hosted by the wineries, at various restaurants. Friday the antiques shops along Royal Street open their doors to a bustling wine and cheese tasting. Saturday there is a full menu of seminars on various food and wine topics, such as old vintage zinfandel, Chardonnay with foods, Chateauneuf du Pape with Louisiana sausage. There are question-and-answer sessions as well as food demonstrations to help you get the most out of your dining in New Orleans experience. Then, armed with recommendations, you're on your own.

GREATER NEW ORLEANS

THE PONCHATOULA STRAWBERRY FESTIVAL

Ponchatoula (North Coast), early April
24182 Hwy. 22, Ponchatoula, LA 70454
Tel. 504/386–6677

From downtown New Orleans take I–10 west to Route 55, which runs into Ponchatoula. Ponchatoula is the antiques capital of Louisiana—more than 200 shops line both sides of Main Street. The area also happens to be famous for its straw-

berries, which seem to know no season and begin appearing in January and February, but are better in April, when the festival celebrates them. The festival is Louisiana's largest two-day fair. Proceeds benefit local nonprofit organizations. Individual booths offer everything to eat—jambalaya, crawfish boil, and shrimp and oyster po'boys. This is a real family fair, with rides, music, and great corny stuff—egg throws, sack races. Ponchatoula strawberries are reputed by their admirers to be the best in the world. Sweet and fat, even in April, they melt on the vine and run red in your hands. The freshly picked berries are trucked in on flats to the grounds at Memorial Park (two blocks from Main Street). After the contest for the best flat of strawberries, the winning flat is auctioned off. You can also buy just about anything having to do with strawberries: jellies, jams, chocolate-covered strawberries, strawberry glaze, and, of course, the berries themselves. These berries need no sugar to make a comforting Strawberry Delight.

STRAWBERRY DELIGHT

1 8-oz. package cream cheese

1 can condensed milk

1 8-oz. package whipped topping

1 tbsp. lemon juice, freshly squeezed

4 pints fresh strawberries, sliced

1 12- or 16-oz. jar strawberry glaze

1 large box vanilla wafers

Mix cream cheese, condensed milk, whipped topping, and lemon juice with electric mixer until mixture is smooth and well blended. Mix sliced strawberries with ¾ of the strawberry glaze. Cover the bottom of a clear bowl with vanilla wafers. Pour ½ the cream-cheese mixture over the wafers. Pour ½ the strawberry mixture over the cream-cheese mixture. Cover the strawberry mixture with a new layer of vanilla wafers. Pour the remaining cream-cheese mixture over the wafers. Pour the remaining strawberries over the cream-cheese mixture. Cover the strawberries with the remaining ¼ of the strawberry glaze. Garnish with large strawberries cut in half. Best chilled before serving.

KLIEBERT'S ANNUAL ALLIGATOR DAY

Hammond (North Coast), August
41083 W. Yellow Water Rd., Hammond, LA 70403
Tel. 504/345–3617

At this alligator open house with the Klieberts, the food is free, plenty of gator is served, and cooking tips are dispensed by the Klieberts. Baby gators hatch live on this day, and knowledgeable guides take you around to see all the gators, from hatchlings to 40-year-old monsters. You can also see turtles—the snapping variety, from which such good

soup is made—marsh nutria, otter, mink, muskrat, and beaver (of which, they say, the tail is so good). There are plenty of hides to buy. Gator steak sandwiches can be had at the deli. You can also purchase various cuts of alligator steak (from the tail, and skinned), but call your order ahead, so it will be ready. To be good, alligator should be of a certain size; ask Jean Kliebert. Get frozen alligator chuck, for *boulettes* (meatballs).

ALLIGATOR SAUCE PIQUANTE

(Recipe by Carl Guillot)

3 lbs. alligator meat, preferably from the tail

3 tbsp. cooking oil

3 tbsp. all-purpose flour

3 medium onions, chopped

2 cloves garlic, chopped

2 no. 2 cans tomatoes

1 6-oz. can tomato paste

2 pints boiling water

3 ribs celery, chopped

6–8 shallots, finely chopped

2 large bell peppers, chopped

4–6 bay leaves

1 tsp. allspice

1 tbsp. sugar

1 lemon, thinly sliced

½ lb. butter

Salt and pepper to taste

Sherry or red wine, optional

Parboil or pressure-cook the meat; tenderizing (pounding it as though it were a veal scallop) helps. Brown flour in oil to make a roux. Add vegetables and tomato paste and cook slowly 30–40 minutes. Add chunks of alligator meat with enough boiling water to cover. Boil and reduce for 30 minutes. Add celery, shallots, green peppers, bay leaves, allspice, and sugar. If desired, sherry or red wine may be added. Raise heat and thicken. Add sliced lemon and butter just before serving. (This recipe for sauce piquante may be used for other kinds of meats, and especially turtle.)

ST. RITA PECAN FESTIVAL

New Orleans (Harahan, a suburb upriver), mid-November
7118 Jefferson Hwy., New Orleans, LA 70123
Tel. 504/737–2915

Held in the schoolyard behind the church, this old-fashioned church fair has rides, booths, tents, bands and dancing, and home cooking. Under the big top you'll find dinner bargain plates of Italian, Creole, and Cajun food—

jambalaya, lasagna, and étouffées. There is also a pecan competition—desserts, pralines, and arrangements are judged and awarded prizes. The Pecan Emporium offers pecans, T-shirts, hats, pecan crafts, pecan jewelry, pecan fudge, and pralines: Everything you ever thought could be done with this nut and more.

PECAN PRALINES

3 cans evaporated milk

¼ lb. butter

8 cups granulated white sugar

8 cups shelled pecan meat

⅓ cup vanilla extract

Combine milk, melted butter, and sugar in a saucepan. Cook on high heat to a rolling boil. Lower temperature to medium and continue to boil for 20 minutes more, stirring constantly. Remove from heat. Add and mix in vanilla. Add pecans and stir until mixture thickens. Turn quickly onto greased foil. Allow to cool.

CAJUN COUNTRY

Le Festival du Poisson Armé (Garfish Festival)

Baldwin, early May

c/o Marie Cole, Box 308, Baldwin, LA 70514

Tel. 318/923–7781

In Baldwin, between New Iberia and Morgan City, you will find a festival where the meat of the gar is celebrated—in ground fish balls and deep-fried fillets. Here are some of the ways the Cajuns prepare an antediluvian fish treat:

GARFISH BALLS

1 lb. ground garfish meat

½ lb. potatoes, boiled and peeled

1 egg

3 shallots, chopped

⅛ cup all-purpose flour

⅛ cup commercial Creole seasoning

⅛ cup corn flour

Oil for frying

Mix first 6 ingredients and roll into bite-size balls. Roll in corn flour and deep-fry until balls float.

FRIED GARFISH

Bite-size pieces of garfish

Tabasco sauce

Salt and pepper to taste

Mustard

Corn flour

Sprinkle Tabasco sauce on fish and let soak for five minutes; add salt and pepper to taste. Add mustard to cover all of fish. Roll in corn flour. Deep-fry until cooked thoroughly.

Now you have your bite out of history, prehistoric and culinary.

LOUISIANA SUGARCANE FESTIVAL AND FAIR

New Iberia, last full weekend in September
Box 97768, New Iberia, LA 70562
Tel. 318/369–9323

New Iberia Parish (the Louisiana equivalent of "County" in the rest of the country) is the largest sugarcane grower in the Sugar Belt. The cane (dark green and 6 feet high) grows right up to the roadside. Many people stop and snap off a piece to suck on as they drive. The Sugarcane Festival celebrates the harvesting of the cane, the second-largest cash crop of Louisiana (behind cotton), with a gross farm value of $448 million in 1995. It's no wonder the Sugar Bowl is played here. The state ranks number two in the nation in production of the plant that was introduced here by the Jesuits, who first grew it successfully behind their church on Baronne Street in New Orleans, whence it spread its wealth throughout the state. The harvest in New Iberia Parish begins on Monday just after this festival. This is the last blowout before the hard work of chopping cane begins, and the local Cajuns pull out all the stops to celebrate. There is a parade and a livestock show. A quilt show is staged, displaying astonishing workwomanship. The World Championship Gumbo Cookoff is held for various categories of entrants, to allow a maximum number of winners, including amateurs and professionals. The best are offered for sale; you can taste the winner for a dollar a bowl. Sit around and eat it as the Sugar Queen is selected from among likely Cajun beauties. There are the Sugar King's luncheon and the Queen's dinner, eating booths, music, dancing, a run; everything associated with a country fair, including a sugar cookery competition that draws rock-candy and sugar-cookie entries, and more, including the tasty morsels that follow:

ORANGE-SLICE CANDY COOKIE

- 1 cup margarine
- 1 cup sugar
- 2 eggs
- 1 tsp. vanilla extract
- 1 tsp. baking powder
- 2 cups all-purpose flour
- 1 tsp. baking soda
- ¼ tsp. salt
- 1 cup light brown sugar
- 1 cup oatmeal
- 2 cups pecans, chopped
- 1 cup orange-slice candy, chopped

Preheat oven to 350°F. Cream margarine and sugar together. In a separate bowl, beat eggs and vanilla. Blend with the creamed mixture. Sift together baking powder, flour, baking soda, and salt. Stir gradually into egg and sugar mixture. Mix well. Stir in brown sugar, oatmeal, nuts, and candy. Drop by tablespoonfuls on ungreased cookie sheet about 2 inches apart. Bake for 10 minutes. Yields about 6 dozen.

INDIAN CULTURE TODAY

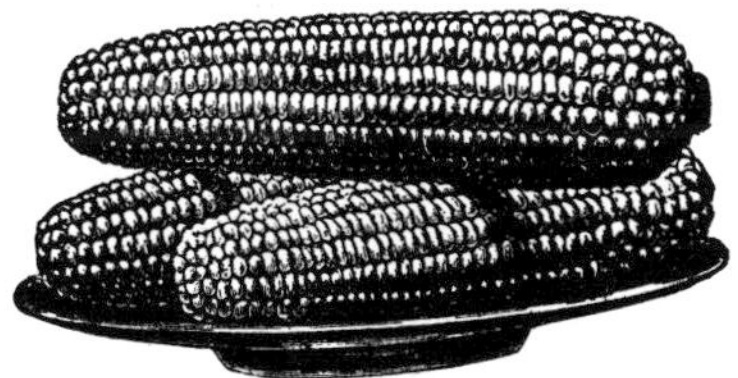

We have seen how the Native Americans along the Mississippi Valley came to terms with their environment, discovered and developed its food resources, and passed this vital know-how to the new settlers. Ironically, it was this knowledge that helped the interlopers to stay. We know the result, and we know what the new Americans gained. For glimpses of how some of the original American cultures, now mostly devastated, prospered and lived, and what they ate and celebrated, there is a food and dance festival reasonably close to New Orleans. Here, you can taste their food and watch their dances. You'll be welcome and even invited to partake of an original cultural experience.

THE FESTIVAL OF CORN

Corn held a special and often sacred spot in Indian life. In some tribes it was worshiped as ardently as was the sun; sac-

rifices were offered to it. Corn gave life to the Indians as they gave life to the plant. In many ways Native Americans celebrate their history with today's corn festivals, which acknowledge the plant that sustains them.

The word "corn" has different meanings depending on where in the world it is used. British usage restricts the word to mean wheat; corn they call maize. When communicating with Americans of European descent, the Indians attempted to solve the problem by using the French word *blé,* and this is what you may see on signposts and circulars announcing the festivals. In any case, the staff of life with the Indians, which blé used to be here, should be taken to mean corn, even though its French meaning is "wheat." The Indians became mixed up with the French through the Cajuns. This in turn produced some interesting food (and semantic) effects.

In the mid-18th century, when the British were rounding up and deporting the Cajuns from their homes in Acadia (Nova Scotia) for religious reasons, they found these French speakers living side by side with the local Indians; they had intermarried, established and exchanged moieties, and become—from the English point of view—hopelessly entangled and enmeshed with them. The British couldn't tell them apart, so they deported them all, Acadians and Indian associates, too. When the newcomers found homes in southern Louisiana, the local Indians—the Natchez and the Chitimachas—welcomed them both. The Crees introduced the Cajuns, and everyone lived in close harmony and in nature. The Indians found the Cajuns could cook, and from the Indians the Cajuns learned the ways of the swamp. They learned the Indian way of making a pirogue, by burning out the insides of a fallen log, and how to sit silently in one and skim the shadows on the surface of the swamp and surprise the animals they hunted there in its waters.

So much were the rural Cajuns accepted by the native peoples that, to this day, when the Indians give a corn festival, there are Cajuns mixed in with it. And so, happily, is their food. In fact, the winner of the corn-cooking contest at one of these festivals was not a corn soup (an Indian favorite) or corn bread (an Indian staple), but corn *maque choux* à l'Acadienne (corn, onions, bell and red peppers), nice and hot and spicy.

THE TCHEFUNCTE POWWOW

The Tchefuncte Campgrounds
Folsom, LA 70437
Tel. 504/796-3654

Put on by the Louisiana Indian Heritage Association, this powwow is held twice a year, generally on the first Friday and Saturday in May and Thanksgiving weekend, to celebrate the bounty of the American harvest. Call the campgrounds for exact times each year. Folsom is just a few miles north of Covington (which is north of Lake Pontchartrain on New Orleans's north coast).

While the dancing goes on to the drumbeat, the tasting committee goes around, and you can, too—visiting the different cooks and demonstrations, asking questions, digesting, and writing down opinions and recipes—before a winner is declared.

There are also fascinating, informative demonstrations of a specifically Indian sign language by men and women in full dress. There was no one Indian language but as many as 2,000 languages spoken by the various tribes. One never knew who one was going to encounter in the forest, and that is why a rich sign language was developed. Miss Indian Princess is selected from a bevy of likely candidates during the traditional dancing. As for the dancing, myriad tribes from all over the state and the country enter their champion teams of dancers. Among them, they have performed all over the world, spreading around an original American art form even older than jazz and the movies. The dances were created to appease the corn god, so he would ensure a good crop. This was serious business—survival. The people were not going to leave it solely up to nature. Like civilizations before and since, they asked for divine intervention. The costumes and paint of the dancers is authentic and beautiful, like nothing you'll see on TV. The feast is more than just food—it's for the eyes and perhaps the soul.

There is a lot of area to explore here; the grounds are about ½ mile long by 200 yards wide and hold about 110 campsites. This idyllic scene pulses with images from long ago and far away—Indian kids swimming in the river, rows of tepees

perched on the bank. You can find crafts and foods all over the village. Bring a bag to buy souvenirs and cooking ingredients on your wanderings and wear comfortable, waterproof shoes. Buy, smell, corn on the cob; it is sweet, spring corn. Taste: You will be surprised at how good it is. This is what the festival is all about.

Other original American foods are also available at special booths throughout the grounds. The corn soup, a highly original variety, contains corn and seasonings and spices. The corn-soup recipe below is provided by Strong Buffalo, a Choctaw-Cherokee who teaches Indian history to Louisiana schoolchildren as well as to itinerant writers.

STRONG BUFFALO'S CORN SOUP

2 cups water, for a small portion
1 bell pepper, chopped
6 shrimp
2 strips bacon, cut up
1 large onion, thinly sliced
1 ear sweet corn

Bring water to boil. Meanwhile, chop onion and bell pepper, chop bacon, and sauté them together in a separate pan. Add shrimp to boiling water. Cut kernels off the ear of corn and add them to boiling water. Add sautéed mixture to pot. (Optional: ½ cup frozen lima beans will make the soup more substantial, and still keep it Native American.)

Indian bread and fried bread are also here; the latter used to be fried corn bread, the "universal Indian food." It started out as cornmeal, according to Strong Buffalo, "ground in a mush, rolled in a ball, and fried with bear fat." This, of course, became hush puppies. Now they are made with regular flour (which shows who won the Indian wars) and fried in vegetable oil. This last shows a Cajun influence, much appreciated by these Indians; after all, bears can't be raised like canola.

Here is a Cherokee recipe for an interesting bread.

CHEROKEE BEAN BREAD

1 gallon spring water
1 cup cooked pinto beans
4 ears sweet corn, in husks

Boil the ears of corn with their husks still on in spring water for 9 minutes. Remove and reserve the husk. Cut off the kernels and mash them. Add the cup of cooked beans and mix. Roll the mass into 2-inch balls. Wrap the balls in corn husks and bake at 300°F for ½ hour. For an extra taste, spread with honey.

Another treat is shrimp on a stick—a whole bunch of 'em, and quite delectable; you can dip them in hot alligator sauce. There's also the alligator: fried on a stick—"an honest half foot of gator," so the hawker says. It's chewy and savory, nothing like chicken, but reminiscent of rubbery bluefish.

Completing the round-up of Indian assimilation and things to eat, there are hotdogs (on a fine spring day they are grilled over a campsite fire and taste as good as at my church fair), barbecue (beef) sandwiches with alligator sauce, crawfish étouffée, and filé gumbo—the kind with sassafras leaves, which makes it a Cajun-Indian delight.

Gumbo, basically a fine fish and vegetable soup, always had a weakness: It was too thin. The Native Americans showed the Cajuns—and Creoles, too—how to make it work by sprinkling on it (after the soup was taken off the heat) the ground powder of mature sassafras leaves. This tree, allied to the laurel, contains a mucilaginous substance that's more aromatic than flour and that works as well as flour as a thickening agent. It makes the gumbo filé, or "run," as Cajun cooks like to call it, and this in a time when flour could not be had. Here is yet another example of the Native American's awareness of nature and the human propensity to experiment and work with it toward the good of the community. And it is how, thanks to this technique, that filé gumbo became a staple of the Cajun, Creole, and entire New Orleans community. You can try this magical thickener in your recipes, too. Bundles of raw sassafras leaves, still on their branches, are available at the fair. The woody strips of bark work wonders also; the aromatic substance is in them as well.

You can stay at the campground; it is like staying in an Indian village. Call the campground for details and rates. Otherwise, it's best to stay in Covington:

BEST WESTERN NORTHPARK INN

625 N. Hwy. 190
Covington, LA 70433
Tel. 800/528–1234

At this nice place, the staff is very helpful and the rooms are large, with crisp modern decor that is more than spartan.

The breakfast is free (Continental); New Orleans is 35 miles to the south, across Lake Pontchartrain.

HOLIDAY INN COVINGTON
501 N. Hwy. 190
Covington, LA 70433
Tel. 504/893–3580

If you are a little sportif, you can enjoy a beautiful outdoor-indoor pool, a whirlpool, exercise equipment, and an after-hours bar and lounge. New Orleans is a half hour away, and a very different world.

The Basket Weavers. You may note, elsewhere, that Louisiana is loaded with Indian tribes that have museums and/or casinos; not all are worth visiting. Less than a two-hour drive from New Orleans, however, is a worthwhile installation in Charenton, Louisiana:

CHITIMACHA RESERVATION
155 Chitimacha Loop, Charenton, LA 70523
Tel. 318/923–4830

Practically across your path on your way to Cajun country, it lies along Louisiana Route 87. The Chitimacha, like many tribes, have a casino. There is something else, though, to make the trip here interesting: the museum-quality Chitimacha baskets that are on exhibit in the tribe's museum, along with pottery and such artifacts as beadwork, feather work, and dugouts. To actually buy the baskets is difficult; normally, their price is by the square inch. However, you can contact the artists themselves: Scarlet and John Darden (Box 341, Charenton, LA 70523, tel. 318/923–4415) and Melissa Darden (Box 952, Baldwin, LA 70514, tel. 318/923–6090).

In Marksville, Louisiana, about 1½ hours from New Orleans and an hour from Baton Rouge you'll find the Tunica-Biloxi Indian Reservation (Hwy. 1 S, Marksville, LA 71351, tel. 318/253–4578). You could combine a trip here with a visit to Cajun country.

A tour of the Indian museum on the reservation, and of the five Indian mounds in the adjacent Marksville State Commemorative Area (tel. 318/253–9546), shows you one of the places in the country where you can see evidence in the landscape of an ancient America.

The civilization of the mound builders in this part of the country arose some 900 years before the Europeans discovered North America. The most impressive characteristic of this culture is the pyramidal mound, built not to cover a burial crypt but to serve as a foundation for a temple or the house of a chief. The builders of lower Mississippi Valley mounds such as those found here were the immediate antecedents of the sophisticated southeastern chiefdoms—the Choctaw, Chickasaw, Creek, Natchez, and others (whose culture is all around you and who are producing this festival)—that so amazed such European explorers as de Soto. Some of the Mississippi mounds were as high as 100 feet and had bases that covered as much as 16 acres. The immensity of the labor involved in building these mounds would be awe-inspiring even in our age of bulldozers and earth movers. The Mississippian peoples, however, did not even possess the wheel or beasts of burden. The mounds were constructed solely by workers who carried every clod of earth in straw baskets. It was a human epic akin to the building of the pyramids of Giza. Specialists agree that the largest of these mounds must have required tens of thousands of people and a few hundred years to build.

Marksville itself is a little light on accommodations; for visitors to the festival, the best bet is to head for the bright lights of neighboring (34 miles northwest) Alexandria.

HOTEL BENTLEY

200 De Soto St.
Alexandria, LA 71301
Tel. 800/356–6835

The 177 rooms in this historic landmark hotel are all quite large, and you're reasonably sure to get one. The entertainment is live, and the food is better than you might expect in a small city. As a grand hotel, it is one of the more expensive moorings in town.

BEST WESTERN OF ALEXANDRIA

2720 W. MacArthur Dr.
Alexandria, LA 71303
Tel. 318/445–5530

The rooms, comfortable and quiet if a little bald, are plentiful. The complimentary breakfast is Continental, so you will still need to eat. You can also take advantage of a landscaped pool, lighted tennis courts, and an oyster bar. A respectable Cajun restaurant-lounge is next door.

ALEXANDRIA TRAVELODGE

1146 MacArthur Dr.
Alexandria, LA 71303
Tel. 318/443–1841 or 800/578–7878

It's just like a midtown hotel. The rooms are clean, comfortable, and simple. There are free coffee and tea service, cable TV, HBO, local calls, and the newspaper.

Loyd Hall Plantation

292 Loyd Bridge Rd.
Cheneyville, LA 71325
Tel. 318/776–5641 or 800/240–8135

For a more homey touch, stay at a bed-and-breakfast on a working cotton plantation, 16 miles south of Alexandria (exit 61 off I–49). Here, with plantation meals, you'll become part of the Old South. Those who stay with the Fitzgerald family are never sorry. Feast on a plantation breakfast, pet their dogs and cats and listen to violin-playing ghosts. There are queen-size suites, fireplaces in rooms, antiques, arrowheads, full kitchens and baths overlooking the pool. It's a sumptuous spot.

At our leisure, we do reflect that we have seen and been with a people who seem to have discovered the secret of being happy with only the bounty of nature. How is this possible? The average urban dweller of today entering the forest woodland would probably anxiously ask of its denizens, how do you eat? The Indian who lived there, from the depths of his experience, would probably answer, how can you starve?

If there is a little of the sleuth or anthropologist in you, visit the remains of one of the country's largest Native American communities at **Poverty Point,** in northeastern Louisiana, just off Louisiana Route 577 near Epps (a five-hour drive from New Orleans). This 3,700-year-old city is part of a state commemorative area, complete with trails and a museum. Upwards of 5,000 people lived within the city's walls. Certainly, it was agriculture and meat-and-fish curing that supported this large population.

The most imposing and mystifying structure at the site is the stupendous, 600-foot-long, 70-foot-high, eagle-shape mound. Another mound, close by, is only slightly smaller. The whole village is surrounded by an earthworks that has survived even into our times. We wonder today at the persistence and patience of the Indians who had to move a calculated ½-million tons of earth with sticks and straw baskets, to build it.

The dominant culture of this Muskogean-language-speaking group of Chickasaw, Choctaw, Creek, Seminoles, and others, which once numbered 50,000, were the Natchez. They were descended from the Aztec and practiced the Aztec ritual of human sacrifice. The Natchez called their chief the Great Sun and were, like the Aztec, ardent sun worshipers. They thought that human sacrifice was the only way to keep the sun rising in the morning and keep the light on. Their neighbors, victims of the sacrifice, objected, but without success.

When the French moved into the area, the commander of the French troops coveted Indian lands for a plantation for himself and ordered the Natchez to move. Instead, of course, they attacked, killing 200 French soldiers. Finally, the Choctaw allied themselves with the French and the Natchez were nearly wiped out. The 400 captives left (including the chief, the Great Sun) were sold by the French into slavery in the West Indies. The few Natchez who survived were gathered up, bandaged, and adopted by other native peoples, but the name Natchez had disappeared except for a dank city on the Mississippi. Remarkably, in 1940, two old people of Natchez ancestry were discovered living among the Cherokee. They still spoke the old language. Though Natchez blood still flows in the veins of some Chickasaw, Creek, Choctaw, or Cherokee, all that remains of that once-awe-inspiring culture are these mighty mounds beside the Mississippi.

Bons Crus and True Brews

Not only can you get jambalaya and a crawfish pie in New Orleans, but you can also savor native wines and native beers to go with whatever you eat.

Bons Crus

Because New Orleanians care about food, it follows that they care about wine. Wine has always been an integral part of a dining experience in the classic Creole tradition. For years it was wondered whether New Orleans could produce a regional wine up to its high dining standards. The topographical, soil, and climatic conditions of the area seemed to distance the idea as a dream beyond reality—the land was too wet, the air too humid, there was too much sun and heat (wine grapes seem to do best in areas where they can barely squeeze out a living). But people are stubborn; the viticulture itch struck around Covington—just the other side of Lake Pontchartrain from Metairie—with first-generation Americans of French and German ancestry. Their wines received awards at the 1885 World's Industrial and Cotton Centennial Exposition, and so there seemed a chance that a wine industry might spring up to fill the New Orleans thirst for the grape. This hope, however, was put under by a pestilence that had nothing to do with record rains or wet soil or any other weather phenomenon, but was in fact man-made: Prohibition. Wineries across the nation went under; those in Louisiana stopped producing as operators went back to more profitable farming.

PONTCHARTRAIN VINEYARDS

81250 Old Military Rd. (Hwy. 1082)
Covington, LA 70433
Tel. 504/892–9742

A young attorney from New Orleans, John Seago, had served with the military in Germany, where the wine bug bit him, as he says. In 1977–78, he "decided to see which French/

American hybrid vines would work" in the rolling hills of the 19th-century Louisiana wine-growing region and "planted some vines at a friend's"—just like that. With the dedication of a few partisans, Pontchartrain Vineyards came into being, and the Louisiana wine industry was reborn.

Now yielding upward of 3,500 gallons per year, Pontchartrain is planted with vines that do better in local climatic conditions, disease-resistant French/American hybrids. It produces Chambourcin (red) and Semillion, Seyval, and Villard white wines and aims to settle down at 2,000 cases a year. The vintner says he is "excited about doing this in Louisiana because you don't fake people out here about good food or wines." He plans to keep much of his produce in the New Orleans area, where it can be featured as a local wine, as that is how many great wines of the world started out. While I was in the area, I was hard pressed to find a drop of it. "There is a demand for it, you know," I was told. Conscious of where it stands, in the latitudes of the world, and where it wants to be placed, a wine to go with Creole food, Pontchartrain fits comfortably in the taste niche of a Southern wine—Rhonelike and chewy, but with a flavorful background of berries.

TRUE BREWS

New Orleans is a beer town. The champagne of Mardi Gras is beer, and a reasonable number of regional breweries once operated from here. Although there are only two remaining, and one operating as a presence, the city still has several brewpubs, wonderful bars, and a fine microbrewery where you see beer being made and sit down to some respectable grub. What is a micobrew? It is a beer from a company whose total production does not exceed 15,000 barrels per year. By comparison, for example, Budweiser produces 86 million barrels—which makes it a megabeer.

Beer is one of the oldest beverages known to humans. It was considered food (and in some parts of the world still is); in ancient Mesopotamia workers were paid partly in beer. In early civilizations, the brewmaster's was often one of the highest positions in the land. He was also the keeper of the grain magazines, the crucial ingredient in beer. Beer is a product of the sugar in plants, as is wine, but in beer the sugar comes from grain, not fruit, and the water is added. Beer is 99% water, so the quality of the water used to make it is extremely important, a fact that is often overlooked. While some breweries go through all sorts of transportation machinations—pipelines and tank cars—to secure the critical commodity, others go to the source and set up operations there. The other critical brewing ingredient—the one that contributes the alcohol—is malt. Malt is barley that has been sprouted and lightly toasted. The growth of the sprouts produces the plant's sugar. Toasting the sprouts fixes and crisps them so this sugar can be extracted. Toasted sprouts taste sweet, like cereal, crunchy and nutty.

The toasted malt is fed into the milling machine and ground. The grinding exposes more surfaces of the malt and also prepares the malt to mix better in solution. It is the first step in production in most breweries. The ground malt is then fed through a chute to a large vessel called the mash tun, where it is mixed, rather rudely, with hot water. Mashing allows the enzymes to break down the starch molecules in the grain, converting them to sugars. Malt gives beer its flavor and color. The spent husks of barley are strained from the mash in a process known as sparging. The resulting liquid, the wort, is transferred to the brewing kettle, a giant boiler (often copper) usually installed in a brick cylinder with a fire (propane- or coal-fueled) underneath. The wort is cooked at a strong rolling boil to a temperature slightly over 212°F. The wort is then allowed to cool. It percolates, leaving the dregs of malt behind after the wort is drawn off by siphoning. (Often, at microbreweries, the dregs are given to a neighboring farmer. They make a nutritious cattle feed.) Bittering and aromatic hops are added. The amount and type of hops added at this stage further determine the eventual taste and aroma of the beer. They also act as natural preservatives.

Hops are the most interesting of plants. If you get the chance to examine them (included in some brewery tours), take it. They come easily apart in the fingers; smell and taste them. They have heads that look like a ball of basil, with deep green leaves surrounding sprigs of seeds that dip down from

HOPS

the center; the plant has a smell and taste of amazing puckerishness. Altogether it is an herb that seems to do for beer what tarragon does for chicken; it gives it the zip of extra character. Hops are found throughout the northern latitudes of the world: in Germany, England, and the northern United States; many first-rate breweries in this country seem to like hops from the northwest Rockies. New Orleans brewmasters favor U.S. sources such as Cascade, Perles, Mount Hood, and Willamette. Beers with a puckerish or dry, zippy quality to their taste are said to be "well hopped." Hops are responsible for the taste a beer finishes with, the lasting impression it leaves in the mouth.

Once the wort has cooled to 64°F, it is pumped into huge vats in the fermentation room next door. Here, yeast is pitched into the wort. The yeast consumes the wort's sugars and in so doing produces alcohol and carbon dioxide in the process called fermentation, the changing of sugar to alcohol. At some Southern breweries, the vats are made of cypress wood. This conversion determines each beer's alcohol level and degree of carbonation. The kind of yeast used differentiates each beer. Top-fermenting yeast (which ferments on top of the tank) is used to make ale, and bottom-fermenting yeast (fermenting on the bottom of the tank) is used to produce lager; and this is the main division in beers.

From the fermentation vat, the beer, no longer wort, is piped into aging tanks, where it remains for the next 5 to 25 days, depending on whether it is to be ale or beer. The constant cold in the aging tank allows the beer's flavors to blend and become mellow. Samples are taken from the tank daily so that no beer is bottled before it is ready. Before bottling, the beer is cold-filtered (not cooked) through a ½-micron filter that traps impurities and remaining yeast. The result is a naturally filtered beer with a clean, clear finish.

It is the above process, without shortcuts, that is used by leading microbreweries.

Ale is a beer that finishes, and is shipped, fast. More time is taken to make lager, which is the German word for "stored." Both styles of beer spend at least four days fermenting. After two weeks of conditioning and filtering, the ale is shipped; the lager stays three weeks more—up to six weeks for a pilsner, which is stored the longest of the lagers and is the most expensive to make.

Of the original beers made in New Orleans, there are two of which you've probably heard. Jackson Beer has moved all its operation to Texas. Jackson Brewery New Orleans is now devoted to mall promotion, not beer production. The other true (as in made in New Orleans) brew, which helped spread the city's reputation far and wide, is Dixie. When New Orleans came into the Union as part of the Louisiana Purchase, the United States established a mint in the city to signify U.S. ownership. To mollify the Creoles and make their transition from French to American smoother, the mint in New Orleans printed the word *dix,* French for 10, on the backs of its new $10 bills. Americans pronounced the word as it would be said in English—with a hard *x*—and from there the jump to Dixie was a natural slip of the tongue. The new word stuck and spread to include the whole South, as does the beer.

Dixie Brewing Company
2537 Tulane Ave. (Mid-City)
New Orleans, LA 70119
Tel. 504/822–8711

The six-story building, one of the few remaining regional breweries in the nation, continues, with its beer, to be a New Orleans tradition and a Southern institution. Insurance regulations have forced the suspension of tours of the historic old building. Though you can still take it in from the outside, it is impossible to see the mammoth old wood vats and other equipment used in the production of Dixie's Jazz Amber Light and Blackened Voodoo Lager; but, of course, you can taste them in the bottle.

Jazz Amber Light, created and meant to fill what was conceived as an existing market niche for a lighter beer with taste, was formulated by Dr. Joseph Owades, a beer consultant who is recognized internationally as the father of light beer. Jazz Amber Light is the result of a challenge to the doctor to deliver to the market a light beer with a full taste spectrum. Brewed with premium choice malts in Dixie's traditional vats of cypress wood selected and cut by German immigrants, Jazz does come up with a richer, more robust flavor than one would expect from a light beer. Nevertheless, Dixie's Jazz has no more calories than other leading light beers.

Satisfied in the light beer department, the company then turned its attention to the other end of the beer spectrum—Blackened Voodoo Lager. As the name suggests, it's a dark beer. How dark? As dark as a porter; almost opaque, but not quite, with highlights of cypress coming through. How does it feel on the palate? The name, says a spokesman, is meant to suggest "fat" (as in Mardi Gras) Louisiana, swamps and Cajun, and the city of New Orleans. Very well; as a beer it is not as heavy as it appears—not fruity, dry, or bitter—but styled after a Munich beer. Five different malts give it a complex, layered taste. The medium hops, Mount Hood and Cascade, help it finish like a malty lager. Voodoo is meant to suggest "the search within oneself," according to a Dixie spokesperson. Still, it is a controversial beer. Texas tried to ban it because of the use of "voodoo" in the name but dropped the idea when Louisiana, in turn, threatened to ban Lone Star. Blackened Voodoo Lager remains the beer of the undead.

There is, however, another brewery tour to take, and the beer itself is excellent.

ABITA BEER

20184 Hwy. 36
Covington, LA 70433
Tel. 504/893–3143

Here is a brewery in a small grove of pines just east of Covington on Route 36. It is Abita's second, a new brewery. The beer started small in 1986 (with deliveries from the back of a pick-up truck—you might say, in Southern parlance, that Abita beer came into town on a load of watermelons), but is growing fast, due to its recognized excellence. Abita has been

voted "Best beer in New Orleans" in several magazine polls, and most better restaurants serve it—I had it first at K-Paul's Louisiana Kitchen. The beer's speedy acceptance and growth from humble beginnings enabled founder Jim Patton to build the state-of-the-art facility that you can tour.

While many other breweries chemically treat their water before brewing, Abita uses theirs straight from the springs. The first brewery produced 1,500 barrels in its initial year. For the first few years it was available only on tap. As Louisiana's first microbrewery, Abita brews its ales and lagers with a regional taste in mind and offers specialty beers throughout the year for seasonal variety. By 1989 the brewery had installed its first bottling line, and Abita beers became available for takeout. Sales have doubled every year since then; the Louisiana market continues to grow, and new markets have been added throughout the southeastern states. Abita is also sold in Boston, where they appreciate a good beer.

Beer-making today has truly become an exercise in international cooperation and taste. Normally, the barley used in Abita is grown in the United States, then sprouted and roasted to company specifications in England. (When English malt is used, as it is sometimes, it comes from the British company of Munton and Fison.) The roasting time determines the color and flavor of the malted barley. A wide range of roasts can be used, from pale, through caramel and chocolate to black patent (burnt like carbon). Yeast is cultured at Abita from strains developed by a German brewing school. Abita selects different strains of yeast out of hundreds available for each beer recipe it develops.

At Abita, beer is made of just four ingredients: water, malt, hops, and yeast. Some breweries also use rice; Abita does not. "Rice is used because it's cheaper than barley," says Kathleen Patton, Jim's wife and partner. "It has starch that can be broken down into sugars, which can be turned into alcohol, but it does not produce a beer with a good 'mouth feel.' It is not what we like."

Two families of hops are also used—bittering and aromatic. Bittering hops are added first, both as a preservative and for flavor. The primary bittering hops used by Abita is Chinook (sounds romantic, doesn't it? Like a salmon churning up the Columbia River). The aromatic hops are used later in the boil to create distinctive flavor and aroma. All this takes meticulous figuring out, and this is how the brewmaster earns his keep. Among the aromatic hops used by Abita are Mount Hood, Perles, and Willamette.

Abita beers are cold-filtered, which prevents a "cooked" taste. Abita never pasteurizes, boils, or adds chemicals to beer.

Instead of using preservatives, Abita ships its beers and ales as soon as they are "finished"; the result is extremely fresh brews, containing only the natural flavors of malt, hops, and fresh, clean water. This is why the company is so popular and why it is growing so fast.

The Abita Brewpub, on Holly Street in downtown Abita Springs, housed in what was the company's first brewery, in a converted donut shop and gas station, has Abita's original brewing tanks. A city-slick cypress-and-slate bar wraps around the room and welcomes you. To enjoy with the spunky food—gumbo, po'boys, pizza—there is the full complement of Abita's regular beer offerings—Amber, Golden, Turbodog—as well as seasonals such as Abita Bock, Purple Haze, and a rotating Brewer's Choice (which changes according to supply). The Brewpub is a good place to drop in before or after Abita's brewery tour. The free tours are on Saturday at 1 and 2 and on Sunday at 1.

These are the choices:

Abita Amber. One of the company's three beers offered all year, from the first glance it pleases with glints of rich amber color showing through the caramel malt. It's a lager with a smooth, generous flavor. The first beer offered by the brewery, it continues to be its best seller.

Abita Golden. The second of the three main beers is a lighter lager. It uses English lager malt, and Mount Hood hops gives it the crisp, clean taste that makes it good with seafood.

Turbodog. The third of the main brews is a dark brown ale of surprising zest, brewed with Willamette hops and a combination of pale, caramel, and chocolate malts. It is sweeter and has a higher alcoholic kick than Amber or Golden and a bittersweet taste, something like a French vanilla roast coffee that may leave you thinking you're drinking a stout. It began at Abita as a specialty ale but developed such a large, devoted following that it soon became one of the company's standard brews. Its amusing appellation is derived from that of a famous English brown ale. In 1990, when Jim and Kathleen Patton were creating the Turbodog recipe, they wistfully remembered Newcastle Brown Ale, or "Old Brown Dog." It's known throughout England as "the dog" because coal miners in Newcastle would politely decline their wives' invitations to tea after work because they had to "walk the dog," they said. Anyone passing the local pub, however, could tell by the number of dogs parked outside how popular the brown ale had become. When the Pattons visited the brewery, they enjoyed its Old Brown Dog ale. On the spot, they decided to create their own dark brown ale but make it a bit peppier than the other dog. When they tapped their first keg, it was apparent to all that their dog was no puppy. Abita's brewer, Brooks Hamaker, immediately christened it "Turbodog." Everyone at the brewery laughed and agreed, and they began shipping kegs to New Orleans. Among their accounts were some of the fanciest restaurants in the French Quarter, and there was a good deal of resistance from haughty sommeliers who objected to listing a dog, however turbo, on the drink menu. Taste prevailed, however, and soon even matrons from the Garden District were calling for their Turbodog. Turbodog is a dark ale, full bodied and strong. Just the thing for walking the dog. Abita's obvious opinion is that all canine brew comparisons will leave its own higher-powered and darker dog the favored.

Abita Bock (also known as Mardi Gras Bock). This is the company's first seasonal beer, available exclusively from January 1, in time for Twelfth Night, to June 1, taking it through the whole Carnival season and its aftermath. It is brewed with Yakima Perle hops with British two-row and caramel malt. The brewer here prefers two-row to six-row because two-row has more protein, which produces a clearer beer. You see, brewing a successful beer takes thought, imagination, and an understanding of the chemistry of plants. All in all, Mardi Gras Bock is not too far in taste from a German Mai

Bock. Its chewy maltyness, full body, and alcohol levels, however, make it a beer not to trifle with.

Wheat Beer. Available from June 1 to September 1, this is a summer beer. It has a distinctive light, fresh taste. It is the Mount Hood hops, they say, that add a slight and sprightly tartness to the finish. It is meant to be served very cold, even over ice. With a wedge of lemon it is very refreshing. It is introduced into the neck of the uncapped bottle and pushed down. The thumb is then clamped tightly down over the opening of the bottleneck, the bottle inverted, and the slice encouraged to drift upward into the bottle proper like a wayward anemone. Then the beer tastes wonderful, lemony.

Purple Haze. This is a crisp, American-style wheat beer to which fresh raspberries are added during the secondary fermentation. With a subtle raspberry tinge, a glorious aroma, and a tartly sweet taste (a little like cranberries), it is a most surprising and refreshing brew. It's currently available only on draft, and only in southern Louisiana.

Fallfest. This Oktoberfest lager is available from September 1 to November 15. Teutonic in style, it is brewed with German Hersbrucker hops and two-row pale, crystal, and chocolate malts. The result is a mouthful—a full-bodied, malty beer with a frothy, long-lasting head and an exquisite light, amber color that makes it beautiful to look at.

Christmas Ale. Rounding out the Abita delivery and tasting calendar, it is available from November 15 to New Year's Eve. As with the best Christmas presents, each year's offering is a unique surprise with no antecedents. Recipes from previous years are never repeated.

A word about Abita's "springs." Yes, there are springs here. Since its days as a Choctaw Indian settlement, Abita's spring water has been recognized and appreciated. The Choctaws settled here because of the water. They named the springs after an ailing, cherished maiden who drank the water and then recovered her health. The perception that the waters could heal spread from the Chocktaws to the Europeans, and in 1854 the springs were "discovered" and the water, according to the *Abita Springs Gazette*, was "noted for the healing of kidney trouble, Bright's disease, liver trouble, dyspepsia and nervousness." In the midst of rolling hills covered with great pines, sweet gum, oak, and magnolia, even Abita's air was delicious. The place became a favorite health resort. The fame of its water spread and won awards for purity. The following item appeared in a 1904 newspaper:

St. Louis, Oct. 15, 1904. – The Bureau of Awards (St. Louis Fair) today granted silver medals and awards of merit to both plain and carbonated Abita Springs water exhibited by the Abita Springs Water Company of Abita Springs, Louisiana. This award carries with it mention of the exceptional purity and the special mineral properties of the water. Hundreds of waters from all over the world were contesting for honors. The honor conferred is an exceptionally high one, and is only given after all waters had been subjected to severe tests.

More recently, Abita Springs has been added to the Louisiana State Parks system. Plans are in motion to improve the grounds and walks and make it one of the state's garden spots. Abita water is bottled and sold as spring water all on its own. The water's chemical composition makes it ideal for brewing beer. Its sodium content, for example, is only 31 parts per million—lower than some famous bottled waters you probably buy; start looking at labels. The water is taken from a 2,000-foot-deep well and tests free from man-made contaminants.

Started in the Northwest, around Washington State and Oregon, brewpubs jumped eastward with amazing alacrity, especially to Vermont, where they flourished, and now they are sweeping the country. The essential idea with beers (especially with ales) is to drink them when they're young and fresh; this is not wine—bottle age adds nothing. It is, in fact, a subtraction in taste. What could be a younger beer than one just made? This is the whole point of a brewpub. You go into a pub and drink beer brewed on the spot. Frequently the pub is very small, but it has an undeniable, authentic charm. Often, you can look through a window or glass wall and see the beer being made. Of course you can smell it; many places are permeated with the smell of the malt. Then the beer is served to you, along with some palatable grub, and you taste the brew at its nascent moment.

Aside from Abita, of Abita Springs, there is a growing number of brewpubs in New Orleans itself, such as:

CRESCENT CITY BREWHOUSE
527 Decatur St. (French Quarter)
Tel. 504/522-0571

The brewhouse is two stories high and hugely successful. Always crowded, it's very welcoming and homey. The decor is mainly brick walls around a concrete floor that goes straight back through to the fermentation room behind the bar, so you can see how the beer is made before you drink it. The bar is oak, with a warm, friendly patina. From the second floor, three huge windows in the wall overlooking the great vats in the fermentation room allow you to watch (and smell) the beer being brewed. Basically Crescent City brews four beers, all malt lagers: Carnival, an unfiltered amber lager with plenty of character (possibly because it is not filtered) and their most popular beer, especially during Carnival; Pilsner, a very hoppy brew, much like its European model and aged, according to classic tradition, for five to seven weeks; Red Stallion, a heavily filtered Vienna-style beer, very smooth, with great head retention, that gives you the feeling, "it's alive!"; and Black Forest, another European, Munich style, mahogany in color, a little smoked in flavor.

Almost as much as for the beer, customers roll in for the food, which is spunky and insolent (the way brewpub food ought to be). Favorites at the bar are the red stallion mussels; these crustaceans are perhaps the ideal companions for beer. Don't ignore the crab cakes, onion rings, nachos, fried calamari, salads of many sorts, soups, sandwiches, pizza, and ratatouille.

Europeans seem to love this place. They are surprised and delighted at the quality of the beer. After they've been in the country a while, they confess to being disappointed with the American national blands. "They come into the Brewhouse," says manager Richard Shultz, "and they discover beer like they're used to drinking in Europe—in England, France, and Germany"—beer with taste and character. Also, the price of the tasteful food is correct.

The following are not breweries or even brewpubs; they are, however, centrally located in New Orleans and worth a visit for a beer or two. They're far more amusing for the true taster than the tinseled remains of the Jackson Brewery; beers listed are generally on tap and always very fresh.

Cooter Brown's Tavern

509 S. Carrollton Ave. (Riverbend)
Tel. 504/866–9104

One of New Orleans's great bars, it can be a home away from home. It's vast—4,000 square feet, with two bars, but it has only 10 tables and 6 booths. The tasty food, self-service (you order and pick it up), consists of spicy boiled crawfish, seafood sandwiches, fried clams, and fried or fresh oysters (the latter served at an oyster bar). There are also two pool tables and an ATM. Cooter's stocks 325 different beers, featuring a great choice of European brews, including the superb and hard-to-find-in-the-U.S. l'Abbayée de Leffe (Belgian). On tap are 42 beers, including five Abitas and two Rickenjax (a new, interesting microbrewery north of Baton Rouge near Jackson, Louisiana; try their Old Hardhead). It's a great place to unwind, and the natives (mostly grad students, and often loud) are friendly.

THE BULLDOG TAVERN

3236 Magazine St. (Garden District)
Tel. 504/891–1516

Bulldog bartender-manager Billy Norris is among the most knowledgeable sources on beer in New Orleans. He has made the Bulldog into one of the most worthwhile beverage stops in the city. Here's why. The bar has 125 beers in the bottle and 50 on tap, with a unique serving concept behind them. The taps glimmer behind the 32-foot bar, gleaming in their polished brass housings, lit up with spotlights, a beautiful sight. (Admire it, and you're sure to get a sigh of sympathy from Billy.) Then you think of it: Each tap draws a different beer. Billy has five of the Abitas on tap—Amber, Golden, Turbodog, Wheat, and a bock. He also draws all three Rickenjax brews: American Ale, ESB (for bitter), and Old Hardhead. The American Ale is the lightest of the Rickenjax family and mildly hoppy. The ESB is hoppier and near red in color. Old Hardhead is a Scottish ale—darker in color and still hoppier. Taste it, and you'll see why it's so named; this is one tough beer. The clatter you hear when you swallow might be your broken teeth on their way down your throat. You can see that a beer this individual could only be made and offered through microbrewery marketing. "Personally, I like 'em; they're all pretty good," Billy says of the Rickenjax. "Kind of new," he says, "but moving quite steadily. We get it very young, when it's just eight days—at the most—old. The whole trick, you know, with beers is to drink 'em while they're young." Billy also proudly draws the beers of the Celis Brewery, in Austin, Texas,

which brews in the wonderful Belgian tradition, argued by critics to be among the best in the world. He can pull two of his brass taps to get these: Celis Grand Cru and Pale Bock. I taste, and I am taken back to the time I first sipped the rich, creamy head of a Belgian beer, in an apartment in Paris. I didn't even like beer, I used to say, up to then.

"People are getting tired of bland beers," says the bartender, "getting turned on to the new stuff. Brown ales, like Turbodog, and the British stuff are the fastest moving." Of course Billy has come up with an imaginative marketing device to keep those customers coming: Taster Cups—1-ounce cups for sipping samples before you plunk down hard cash for a whole glass, which goes up to $4.75 (for a German double bock). "It's worth it," says Billy. "You've got to consider the amount of alcohol you're getting." Some Belgian beers go up to 35 proof. At the Bulldog, you can get more than you pay for.

AFTERWORD

We have pinned down the ancient sources of New Orleans food, sniffed them out, and tasted them. As we have seen, from the time of the Indian, food in America has been the object of intensive search, sacrifice, and even veneration. In our day it has become a mere obsession. It is certainly worthy of travel.

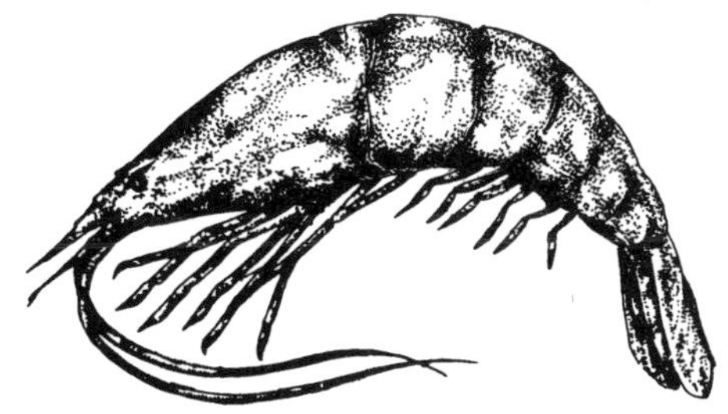

Why do we eat like we have in New Orleans? It obviously isn't to grow on, except maybe in a circum-equatorial way. It might, however, serve as a balm, as a sop for our stress. It is undeniable, however, that food has an entertainment value. It may be that the theater is struggling, but restaurants are booming. In New Orleans they are entertainment in themselves.

To sit in a dining room at Arnaud's, the Commander's Palace, or Brennan's is to sit in a theater; food is offered on the most precious and ornamental of plates by hands schooled in its artful presentation. They could be the hands of an Aztec priest offering what is venerated in itself, for only after worship can it be eaten. Then it is sprinkled with magical spirits and elixirs. The words of its preparation come like incantations. Just when the interest level is highest, it is ignited and glows with an awful blue presence. You feel like Marco Polo, traveled to new, exotic ends of the earth, and seated before the god of food in a new world.

The miracles don't stop. There are soups of creatures undreamed of to savor. Sauces that taste and smell like a whole forest of trees. We have visited more than a different food country, but a different planet, chock-full of new flora and fauna deliciously prepared. Rather than mull over the mystery, we have been encouraged by the denizens to join in with new miracles of taste that know no bounds.

Eat—I should say, dine—and enjoy, and, as the Cajuns say, *"Laissez les bons temps rouler"* (let the good times roll). What could be better than . . .

crawfish pie
pompano en papillote
filé gumbo
and a café brûlot?

If you know what you want, in New Orleans you are certain to get it.

MAPS

NEW ORLEANS

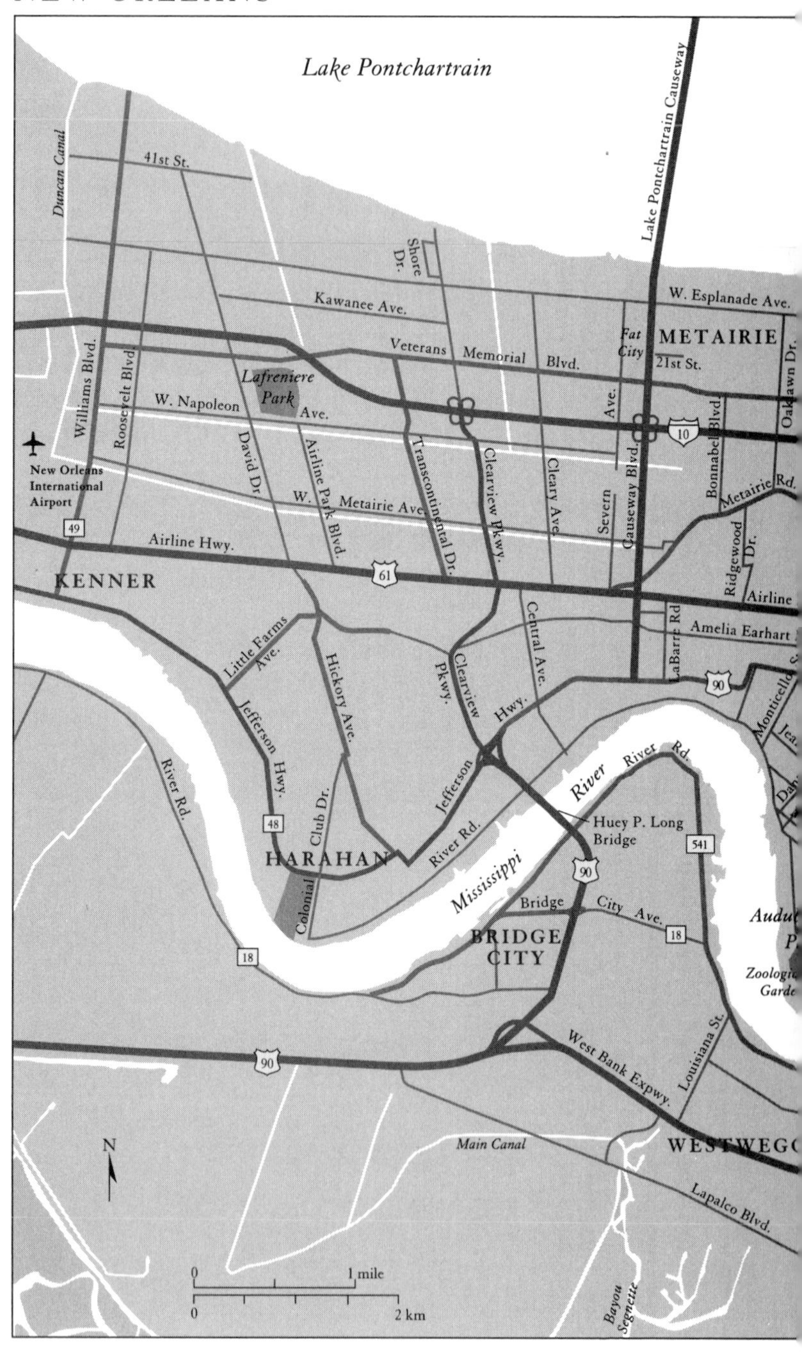

Lake Pontchartrain
Lake Pontchartrain Causeway
Duncan Canal
41st St.
Shore Dr.
Kawanee Ave.
W. Esplanade Ave.
Fat City
METAIRIE
Veterans Memorial Blvd.
21st St.
Oaklawn Dr.
Williams Blvd.
Roosevelt Blvd.
Lafreniere Park
W. Napoleon Ave.
Ave.
Bonnabel Blvd.
10
New Orleans International Airport
David Dr.
Airline Park Blvd.
Transcontinental Dr.
Clearview Pkwy.
Cleary Ave.
Severn
Causeway Blvd.
Metairie Rd.
W. Metairie Ave.
Ridgewood Dr.
49
Airline Hwy.
61
KENNER
Airline
Amelia Earhart
LaBarre Rd.
Central Ave.
Little Farms Ave.
Hickory Ave.
Clearview Pkwy.
90
Monticello
Jefferson Hwy.
Jefferson Hwy.
River Rd.
River
River Rd.
River Rd.
Huey P. Long Bridge
541
48
Club Dr.
HARAHAN
River Rd.
90
Mississippi
Colonial
Bridge City Ave.
18
BRIDGE CITY
18
Zoologic Garde
90
West Bank Expwy.
Louisiana St.
N
Main Canal
WESTWEGO
Lapalco Blvd.
0
1 mile
0
2 km
Bayou Segnette

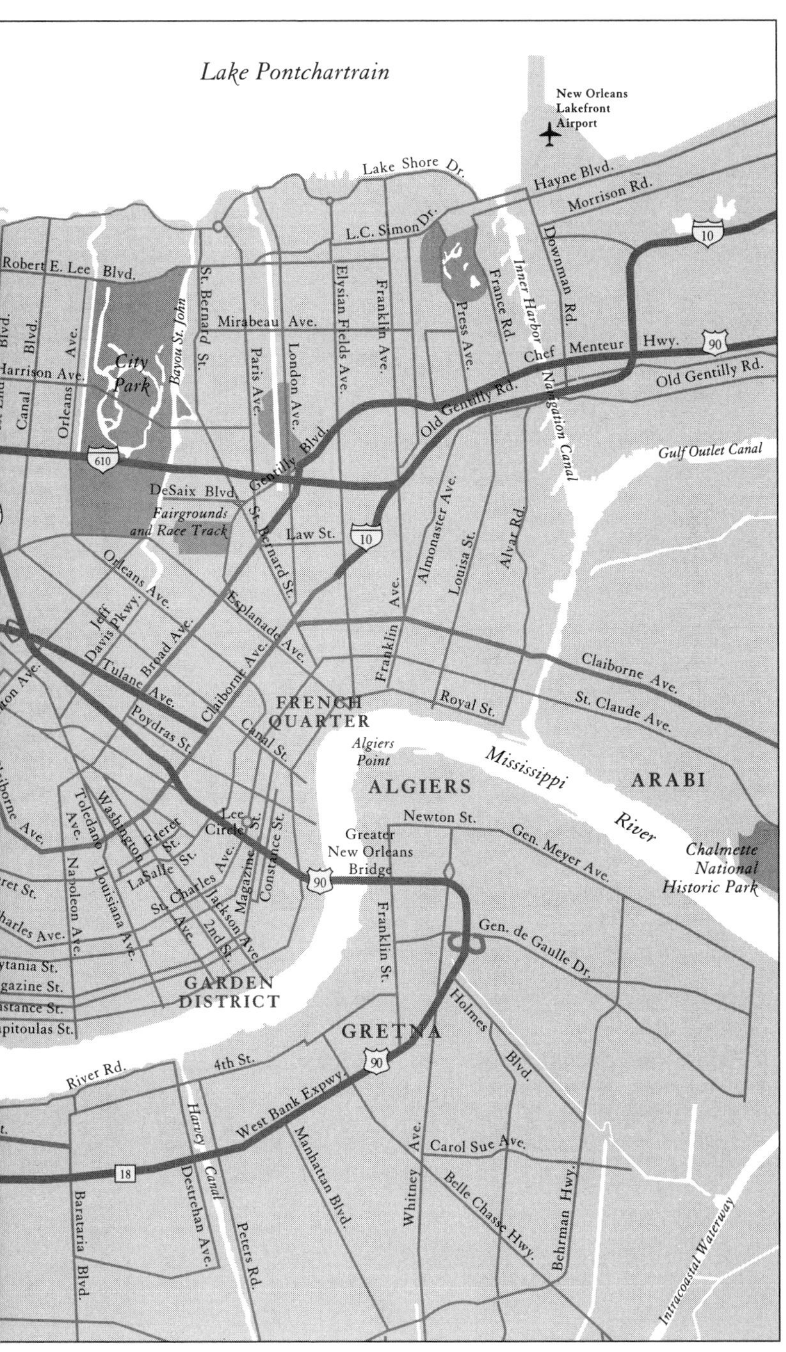

Lake Pontchartrain
New Orleans Lakefront Airport
Lake Shore Dr.
Hayne Blvd.
Morrison Rd.
L.C. Simon Dr.
Robert E. Lee Blvd.
Mirabeau Ave.
City Park
Bayou St. John
St. Bernard St.
Paris Ave.
London Ave.
Elysian Fields Ave.
Franklin Ave.
Press Ave.
France Rd.
Inner Harbor Navigation Canal
Downman Rd.
Chef Menteur Hwy.
Old Gentilly Rd.
Harrison Ave.
Canal Blvd.
Orleans Ave.
Gentilly Blvd.
Gulf Outlet Canal
DeSaix Blvd.
Fairgrounds and Race Track
Law St.
Almonaster Ave.
Louisa St.
Alvar Rd.
Orleans Ave.
Jeff Davis Pkwy.
Broad Ave.
Tulane Ave.
Esplanade Ave.
Claiborne Ave.
Royal St.
St. Claude Ave.
FRENCH QUARTER
Poydras St.
Canal St.
Algiers Point
ALGIERS
Mississippi River
ARABI
Toledano Ave.
Washington
Lee Circle
Newton St.
Greater New Orleans Bridge
Gen. Meyer Ave.
Chalmette National Historic Park
Napoleon Ave.
Louisiana Ave.
Felicity St.
LaSalle St.
St. Charles Ave.
Jackson Ave.
Magazine St.
Constance St.
2nd St.
Franklin St.
Gen. de Gaulle Dr.
GARDEN DISTRICT
GRETNA
Holmes Blvd.
River Rd.
4th St.
West Bank Expwy.
Harvey Canal
Manhattan Blvd.
Whitney Ave.
Carol Sue Ave.
Belle Chasse Hwy.
Behrman Hwy.
Intracoastal Waterway
Barataria Blvd.
Destrehan Ave.
Peters Rd.
610
10
90
18

THE FRENCH QUARTER

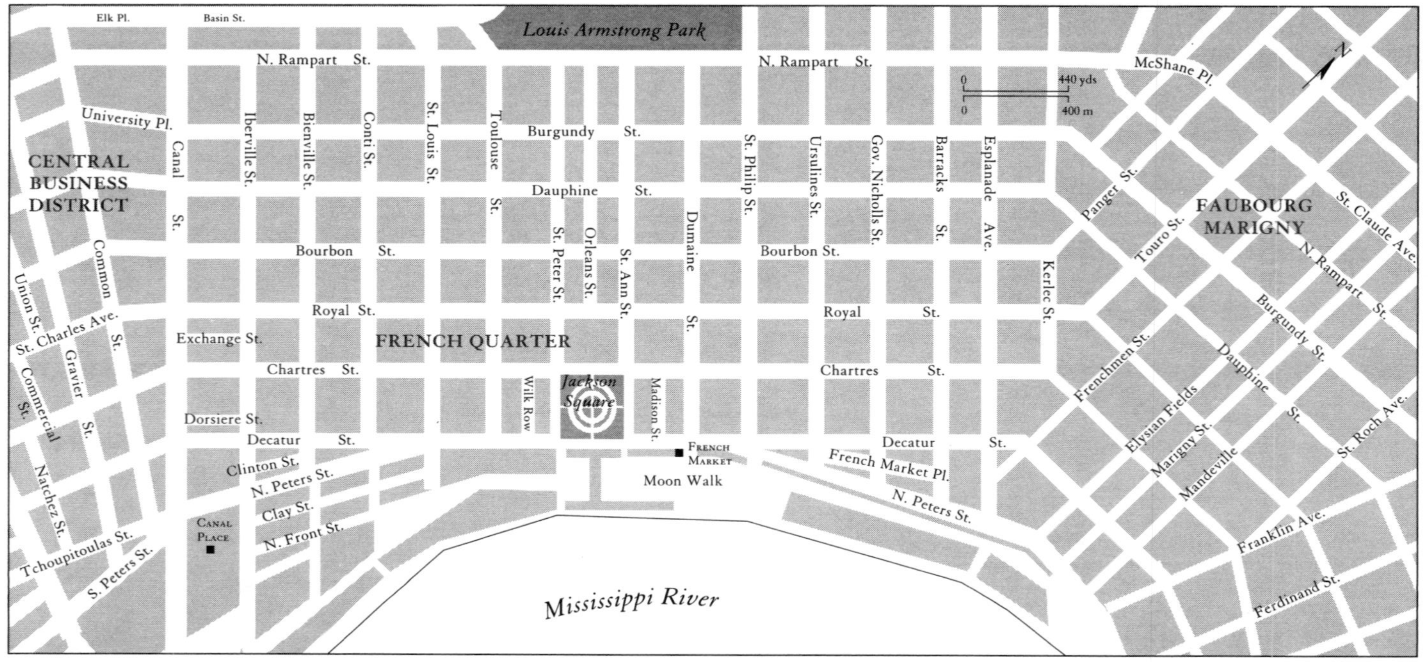

RIVER ROAD PLANTATIONS

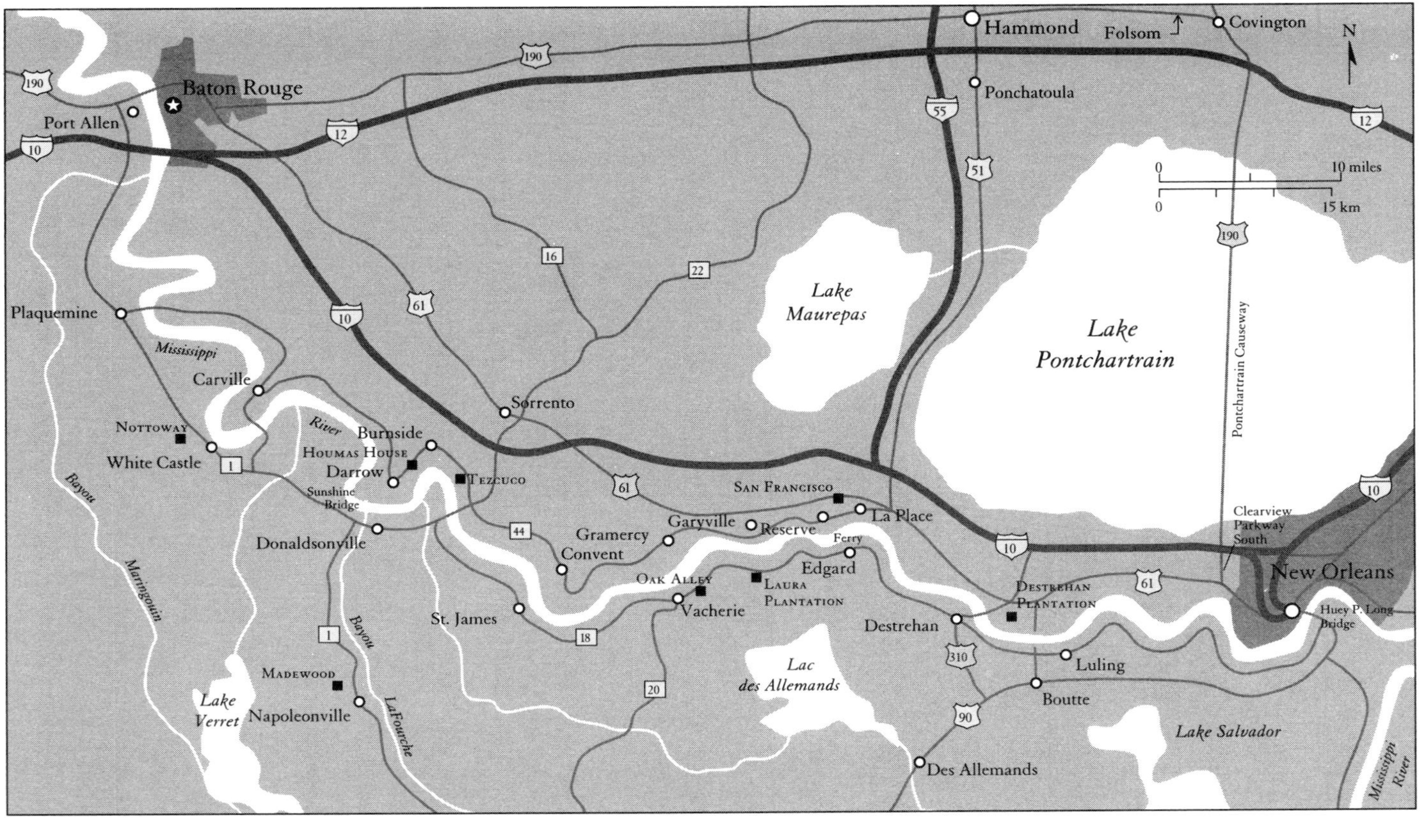

CAJUN COUNTRY

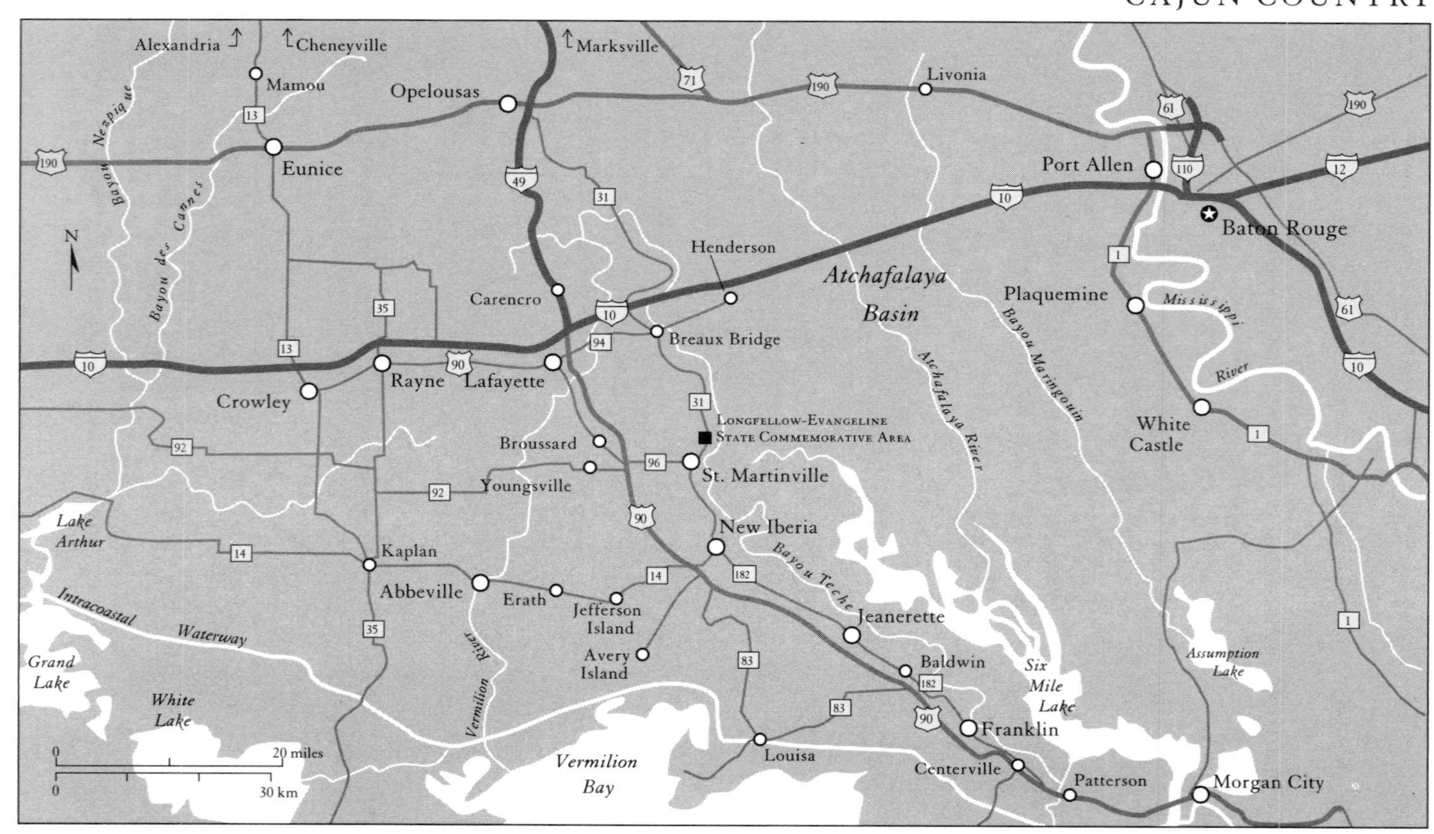

INDEX

INDEX

NOTES

NOTES

NOTES

NOTES

NOTES

NOTES

NOTES

NOTES

NOTES